SHELLEY'S POETRY OF INVOLVEMENT

MACMILLAN STUDIES IN ROMANTICISM

G. Kim Blank
WORDSWORTH'S INFLUENCE ON SHELLEY

Stephen Bygrave
COLERIDGE AND THE SELF

Roland A. Duerksen
SHELLEY'S POETRY OF INVOLVEMENT

David Morse
AMERICAN ROMANTICISM, Volume 1:
From Cooper to Hawthorne
AMERICAN ROMANTICISM, Volume 2:
From Melville to James

John Turner
WORDSWORTH: PLAY AND POLITICS

Andrew J. Welburn
POWER AND SELF-CONSCIOUSNESS IN THE POETRY OF
SHELLEY

Further titles in preparation

Shelley's Poetry of Involvement

Roland A. Duerksen
Professor of English
Miami University, Ohio

MACMILLAN
PRESS

First published 1988

Published by
THE MACMILLAN PRESS LTD
Houndmills, Basingstoke, Hampshire RG21 2XS
and London
Companies and representatives
throughout the world

Typeset by Wessex Typesetters
(Division of The Eastern Press Ltd)
Frome, Somerset

Printed in Hong Kong

British Library Cataloguing in Publication Data
Duerksen, Roland A., 1928–
Shelley's poetry of involvement.
1. Poetry in English. Shelley, Percy
Bysshe—Critical studies
I. Title
821'.7
ISBN 0–333–46068–5

To Mary

Contents

Preface

My attempt in this book is to give readers as clear and direct an account as possible of the spirit or motivation behind the poetry of Percy Bysshe Shelley. This motivation is, as I see it, invariably the impulse of a desire to define and enhance our humanity. And humanity, for Shelley, both originates in and is brought into practice by the human mind itself. While it is individual in its source, it immediately becomes social in its application. Not unheedful of the need for structures in society, the individuality of Shelley's humanity always gives his art itself the quality or energy to deconstruct what has come to be taken for granted and to insist upon the creatively imagined way of knowing. Although my approach to this attainment of humanity in Shelley's poetry is by three paths of emphasis, the primary import throughout centres on the synthesis of the three that is accented in the final chapter.

Though now considerably revised and extended, two segments of the book have appeared earlier in print. A part of Chapter 2 was published as an article in *Bulletin of Research in the Humanities*, and a part of Chapter 5 appeared in *Studies in English Literature*. I wish to thank the editors of both journals for the permission to use these materials in their revised form.

To Miami University I express my thanks for a semester's leave to work on the book, and to my colleagues in the English Department I am grateful for their taking up the slack in teaching duties during my leave as well as for their encouragement.

Oxford, Ohio   R.A.D.

1

Introduction

Approximately fifty years ago, Carl Grabo predicted that 'Shelley's rightful place as a thinker will not soon or readily be accorded him' (vi). That prediction has been proven essentially correct. Although critics have become increasingly aware of Shelley's emphasis on intelligent responses to what is happening in the world, the reading public continues far too pervasively to hold a distorted, obscured view of his poetry in what Grabo calls a 'haze of emotional speculation' that falsifies the essential Shelley. Grabo asserts that 'if ever a man lived the intellectual life . . . it was Shelley' (vii), and more recently Jerome McGann has declared Shelley to be 'the most intellectually probing of all the later Romantics' (118). The necessity now is to establish, as clearly and strongly as possible for the reading public, the fact of Shelley's intellectual power and to make clear and unmistakable its rightful character.

Recent critics have occasionally had difficulty recognizing the coalescent and comprehensive quality of Shelley's emphasis on mental awareness in poetry. In his article, 'Shelley as Philosophical and Social Thinker', Kenneth Neill Cameron, while making a strong case for Shelley as clear-eyed and incisive in his political thought, down-plays the views of those critics who have focused on Shelley's increasing emphasis on the role of love and imagination as constituents of intellect. More recently Harry White has argued that Shelley came to see politics and morality as incompatible but that he remained mendaciously dedicated to both. White, it seems to me, forces Shelley's works into a materialistic box of rationalism that makes no allowance for the mental process (both individual and social) that, united with love, can in Shelley's view be the essence of creative revolution.[1] My intention in the present study is to show, simply and with only the requisite analysis, that Shelley emphatically asserted responsible thought, love and socio-political action to be, if not synonymous, at least indissolubly linked in a continuum.

The mind is, indeed, for Shelley the locale of essential revolution – as it is of all genuinely imaginative productions. And there is for

1

him no discrepancy between the role of the mind in responding
to moral urgings toward liberty and its role in creating new means
of achieving on the actual political level the ends thus engendered.
Shelley is the first creative artist writing in the English language to
propose the method of civil disobedience (non-violent resistance)
as the way to deal in a revolutionary manner with immediate
despotic conditions while the mind is already and concomitantly
working toward higher levels of social existence that would make
despotism itself obsolete.

Not that these concepts of the mind and of its elemental power
in the world were entirely original with Shelley. Though indeed
highly original, he is among the most assimilating and judiciously
eclectic thinkers and writers of our literary heritage. Of particular
importance to his thought were the mental giants of ancient Greece,
among them Socrates, Plato, Aeschylus, Homer, Pindar, Sophocles
and Euripides. Of these, although Aeschylus provided a particular
inspiration for *Prometheus Unbound*, Socrates may be singled out as
the ancient Greek whom Shelley honoured most for his mental
power and for what he taught concerning the human mind. In a
letter Shelley says of Socrates, 'I conceive him personally to have
presented a grand & simple model of much of what we can
conceive, & more than in any other instance we have seen realized,
of all that is eminent & excellent in man', and goes on to laud 'the
fountain of his profound yet overflowing mind' (*Letters*, 2. 145–6).
Summing up an analysis of Greek literary influence on Shelley,
Timothy Webb asserts that 'behind it all was the figure of Socrates,
whom Shelley often associated with Christ as the most perfect of
men, an example by which we might learn to live our own lives
with courage, clarity of mind and self-controul'.[2]

From among modern thinkers whose works Shelley assimilated
into his own thought with varying degrees of enthusiasm and
critical response, there may again be singled out one person in
particular: William Godwin. Others of the moderns who must be
acknowledged as having an important bearing on Shelley's thinking
are Francis Bacon, Jean-Jacques Rousseau, John Locke, David
Hume, Sir William Drummond, Mary Wollstonecraft, Thomas
Paine and Leigh Hunt,[3] not to mention the considerable influence
of two older-generation Romantic poets, William Wordsworth and
Samuel Taylor Coleridge. Early in the process of his assimilation
of insights from these various sources, Shelley was introduced to
Godwin's *Enquiry Concerning Political Justice* (1793), a work whose

influence on his thought and art it would be hard to overestimate. P. M. S. Dawson devotes the major part of a lengthy chapter to a perceptive analysis of Shelley's debt to and affinity for Godwin and makes the important point that Shelley responded with enthusiasm to Godwin's ideas because most of them were already aspirations of his own (77). Godwin, Socrates, and the many other creative thinkers whom Shelley read should be kept in mind throughout the present study as forming an important base upon which Shelley develops his own view of mind and individual imaginative responsibility.

As John W. Wright points out, Shelley maintained that we know only what our minds attend to (22). Holding this definition of knowledge, Shelley is aware that attentiveness of the poet's mind is the prime determinant of great poetry. He realizes that to know what is happening to people and what the happenings mean is the essence of all poetry that matters. Convinced that, as thinkers, poets need to attend to the events of life as they observe them, he recognizes that they have a responsibility to tell of these events as imaginatively and insightfully as they can. For him the primary aim of poetry is to awaken people to their situation, both individually and collectively, and to enable them to discover tendencies and potential consequences in what is happening to them and around them.

In *A Defence of Poetry*, his prose commentary on the potentiality of creative thought in society, Shelley declares that a poet

> not only beholds intensely the present as it is, and discovers those laws according to which present things ought to be ordered, but he beholds the future in the present, and his thoughts are the germs of the flower and the fruit of latest time. Not that I assert poets to be prophets in the gross sense of the word, or that they can foretell the form as surely as they foreknow the spirit of events: such is the pretense of superstition which would make poetry an attribute of prophecy, rather than prophecy an attribute of poetry.[4]

The attribute of poetry that Shelley calls prophecy is a matter of love, of imaginative identification with people, of political concern in the best sense of the term.[5] It is an involved and caring knowledge of things that are – a perception of what constitutes the moving spirit and the tendency behind these present things.[6]

To perceive this spirit and not to reveal it for what it is would be simply unpoetic; it would be the abdication of the poet's most noble duty and most essential aspect. At the very outset of *A Defence of Poetry*, Shelley identifies imagination as the 'perception of the value of those qualities' that are identified by reason. The term *value* has an importance here that is too easily overlooked. Shelley's point, as Wright has noted, is that 'it is first and finally only about values that man thinks' (18). That this thinking about values unavoidably leads the poet to love, to identify imaginatively with others, is expressed in the *Defence* as follows:

> Poetry . . . awakens and enlarges the mind itself by rendering it the receptacle of a thousand unapprehended combinations of thought. . . . The great secret of morals is Love; or a going out of our own nature, and an identification of ourselves with the beautiful which exists in thought, action, or person, not our own. A man, to be greatly good, must imagine intensely and comprehensively; he must put himself in the place of another and of many others; the pains and pleasures of his species must become his own.   (487–8)

Throughout his greatest works, Shelley adheres to the simple but profound principle that poetry, the product of the responsible mind's creativity, educates the poet and others by serving as a means of reaching out, of identifying, and of responding to values newly found in thoughts, events and persons. Akin to this emphasis is Shelley's view that the human mind can reassume a simple and direct way of responding to, and of benefiting from, experience. 'Poetry', he says in the *Defence*, 'lifts the veil from the hidden beauty of the world and makes the familiar objects be as if they were not familiar' (487). Dawson (217) uses the phrase 'primal immediacy of vision' to define this concept and suggests that it reflects the influence of both Wordsworth and Coleridge. Shelley's urging of both a wide scope of imaginative identification and an originality that discards reliance on mere familiarities places a primary reliance on the mind's responsibility.

Though the influence of William Godwin on the development of Shelley's view of the responsible mind is beyond question and is acknowledged as a basic premise in this study, the limit of its extent needs to be noted. Dawson suggests that, by the date of the *Defence*, Shelley had already gone beyond Godwin's moral philosophy[7] – a philosophy that Dawson likens to a Benthamite balance sheet on which the plus and minus qualities of actions are evaluated according to degrees of pleasure and pain (229). His epistemology being in the empiricist tradition of Locke, and having learned from Helvetius as his immediate mentor (Dawson, 82), Godwin developed an empirical, rationalistic view of 'knowledge' that could not be accommodated to the wisdom of Shelley's 'identification of ourselves with the beautiful which exists in thought, action, or person not our own'. By his arrival at this knowledge of imaginative identification with others, Shelley, in Dawson's view, 'transforms Godwin's demand for disinterestedness into the imperative of benevolence' (228–9). Godwin's perspective, derived from that of Helvetius in linking benevolence with self-interest, cannot give satisfactory support to either disinterestedness or benevolence and thus must prove no longer satisfying to a thinker such as Shelley, who is deeply concerned about the need for benevolence.

As Dawson has shown (230, 234), William Hazlitt, like Shelley a disciple of Godwin, very likely helped Shelley toward his concept of the moral imagination. Since Shelley desired to be a moral reformer as well as a poet, he can scarcely have failed to be excited by the crucial role that Hazlitt, in his *Essay on the Principles of Human Action* (1805), assigns to the imagination.[8] Going considerably beyond both Godwin and Hazlitt, Shelley asserts the responsibility of altruistic benevolence to be identical with moral (that is to say, creative) imagination.

As has been amply reiterated by critic after critic since the publication of *The Deep Truth*, a pioneering treatise by C. E. Pulos, Shelley is a sceptic of the first order. Since, then, the values he seeks and advocates cannot be based on a belief in any ultimate, knowable truth, they must be generated in the very processes of human thought, whose subject they are. The responsibility of the individual mind is enormous, but so are the rewards of the mind's freedom from codified and imposed values. Having come to the realization that ultimate truth from some outside source is not available, the sceptic is left to his own mental resources. Shelley finds this to be an exhilarating challenge to the improvement of the human condition – especially since he recognizes thought as the essential business of the poet.

The responsible, thinking poet who necessarily deals with values must, in Shelley's view, create poetry that concerns itself with intellect, with the realm of thought itself. As indicated by the second of the above-quoted passages from the *Defence*, genuinely creative thinking cannot remain self-centred and therefore soon leads to love. Poetry, then, that deals with intellect, will inevitably encompass the subject and express the quality of love. In so doing, it goes out and involves itself in society and its concerns, thus becoming social or political art.

Virtually every one of Shelley's better poems contains elements of all three emphases – intellect, love and social enlightenment – and it is often not easy to designate a given work as dealing primarily with one or the other of these emphases. Nevertheless, an aim of the present study is to do just that. Admittedly, the divisions made in this study are only critical devices. In no way intending to deny or detract from the synthesis that everywhere underlies Shelley's work, I simply find it expedient to discuss individual poems in the context of one or the other of the principal components of what Shelley saw as the poet's role and responsibility. The divisions under which I discuss the individual poems are not intended as inherent separating aspects of the poems themselves but, rather, as devices by which to emphasize elements of the synthesis that pervades Shelley's poetry. My study seeks to show that the three elements cohere in Shelley's ultimate, unified goal of putting the poet and reader in vital contact with the events of life itself, so that their minds may interact with and have an impact upon the spirit and direction of these events. And I find no discrepancy between Shelley's poetic purposes and his very practical social and political thinking.[9] In other words, the study aims to show that Shelley's poetry focuses consistently on the mind's role as creator of the kind of life that is to be lived.

Permeating and interrelating Shelley's poems are two elemental premises upon which he builds his thought: (1) The freedom of the individual mind to make its own choices and (2) the mind's responsibility to recognize and to promote the basic equality of all human beings.[10] As the element linking these two necessities, love is, for Shelley, a meaningful concept precisely because he sees it as a quality or essence generated from within the individual mind. It must not be barred, he insists, by any class, social or economic distinctions from being extended toward any and all individuals anywhere at any time. The poetry clearly reveals Shelley's aware-ness that the creative task is difficult in a world that considers such thinking utopian, idealistic and even dangerous. Yet, assured in his mind that the need to improve the quality of life should be the primary aim of all thought and action, Shelley sees and unhesitatingly accepts his poetic endeavour as a means to the end of enlightening human beings to the challenges as well as the joys of responsible creativity.

Attempting not to lose sight of so important and primary an aim in Shelley's poetry, I shall, in this study, divide the discussion of the poems into the three categories of emphasis mentioned above – intellect, love and social enlightenment – and shall add a fourth category for the works that I have selected for a special focus upon the synthesis of the other three categories. This synthesis, though, as I have already noted, is an important element throughout the poetry, and the categorical designations are intended mainly to mark more clearly the elements of Shelley's thought and to facilitate discussion of the poems.

2

The Emphasis on Intellect

Shelley's short essay 'On Life' is essentially an essay on the all-importance of thinking. Twice in the course of its few pages, he asserts the fundamental philosophy of Berkeley that 'nothing exists but as it is perceived' (476, 477). Defining each individual mind not as a really separate entity but, rather, as a portion of 'the one mind', he yet, following Hume's philosophy,[1] acknowledges that 'mind, so far as we have any experience of its properties . . . , cannot create, it can only perceive'. In the light of Shelley's repeated assertion of the Berkeleyian view that to perceive is to define existence, the word *only* suggests not limitation or diminution, but rather, a precise definition or identification of function. Shelley defines the word *thing* as denoting 'any object of thought, that is, any thought upon which any other thought is employed, with any object of distinction' (478). Since, then, a thing does not have objective existence except as it is perceived, and since it is really a 'thought' useful to other or related thoughts, the question of the substantive origins of things is not nearly so important as is the role of the mind in correct perception.

An indication of the extent to which Shelley sees the mind as identified with life itself is his beginning the final paragraph of the essay with the question, 'What is the cause of life?' and answering it at the end in terms of 'the cause of mind'. Thus it appears that he is more successful than David Lee Clark (*Shelley's Prose*, 171) finds him to be in reconciling Berkeleyian idealism with the scepticism of Hume.

The problem with what people call the reality of life, says Shelley, is that it is usually premised upon the function of a mind that has been deprived of 'that freedom in which it would have acted but for the misuse of words and signs, the instruments of its own creation' (477). Words, images, and symbols are what the mind creates; they are the stuff of perception – which, after all, gives things objective existence for the individual. Not to be subject to mere acceptance and reiteration of handed-down words and signs but instead to respond with honesty and originality of thought to things in one's universe is to be genuinely alive. True, responsible perception is in Shelley's view all the creation that is needed.

As Clark points out (*Shelley's Prose*, 171), the 'Essay on Life' is consistent in thought with other of Shelley's compositions from 1812–14. Too often overlooked in discussions of the early-1812 'Address to the Irish People' is its central premise: 'People have learned to think, and the more thought there is in the world, the more happiness and liberty will there be' (*Shelley's Prose*, 45). In close accord with the theme of 'Essay on Life', the 'Address' makes the logical application of the theme by urging the Irish Catholic workers to 'employ resistance of the mind, not resistance of the body' (*Shelley's Prose*, 46). But this consideration takes us into the area of Shelley's concern with social enlightenment – the subject of a later chapter. In the present chapter our concern is with the emphasis on intellect as expressed in the poetry.

Shelley had written only a few noteworthy poems before he composed 'Mont Blanc', the poem in which he confronts head-on the question of the human mind's role, relative to the world of material things, in the generation of reality. In conjunction with the three other poems that appear with it in one manuscript notebook and that are also concerned with the mind's important place in life, 'Mont Blanc' provides an ideal focal point for the beginning of our study of Shelley's emphasis on intellect. And it may be best dealt with in a context involving also the other three poems that appear in the notebook.

Early valuators notwithstanding,[2] the above-mentioned notebook, which was among the Scrope Davies papers discovered in 1976 at Barclay's Bank, London, is of considerable value, especially for our understanding of Shelley's thinking in 1816 about the importance of human intellect. The four manuscript poems contained therein have an interrelationship that not only enhances the appeal of the two new sonnets among them,[3] but also, in correlation with the variant portions of the other two poems, 'Mont Blanc' and 'Hymn to Intellectual Beauty',[4] adds clarity to our reading of these well-known works. All written during the summer of 1816, which Shelley, Mary Godwin and Claire Clairmont spent with Byron at Lake Geneva, the four poems may be studied as two sets – a sonnet and a longer poem in each set – according to two interrelated and mutually strengthening themes that have to do with the mind and creativity.

The notebook's first poem, an untitled sonnet, and its last poem,

'Mont Blanc', which is only tentatively titled in the notebook,[5] are thematically linked by their mutual involvement with the question of the mind's relationship to the strength of nature. The second and third poems, the sonnet 'To Laughter' and the lyric 'Hymn to Intellectual Beauty', both have as dominant theme a probing of the essence of human value. The notebook may then be seen as presenting, in its first and last poems, an outer or encompassing theme of the mind/nature relationship and as dealing, in the two middle poems, with the consequent or inherent central theme of the end that is to be served by the intellect in its proper relationship to nature.

Considering first the outer, encompassing theme, we find in 'Mont Blanc' an emphatic opening assertion about the interrelationship of the intellect and the material world – the flowing 'universe of things'. The poem, through dramatic narration, asserts progressively that the mind's own contribution, the stream of conscious thought, is ultimately more important in the creative process than is the stream of empirically discernible things. This idea is elemental also in the first sonnet in the Davies notebook. In 'Mont Blanc' the poet-narrator is increasingly aware that his own, his 'human mind' (symbolized by the ravine of the Arve, which is of course materially continuous with what there is at the mountain's peak), cannot rely (at least not solely) on otherworldly, mystical codes or intuitions but must make its decisions by taking into account all that can, and also what perhaps cannot, be known about the universe of things. As Webb makes clear (141), Shelley's 'Mont Blanc' runs counter to the kind of evidence-of-the-hand-of-God poetry that is found in Coleridge's 'Hymn before Sunrise', a poem inspired by the same scenery (though not by Coleridge's actually having seen it), one that Shelley almost certainly had read in *The Friend*.

The 'awful doubt' taught by the mountain leaves place for only a very 'mild', non-dogmatic kind of faith that somehow mankind's contention with nature is worthwhile and good. Although the newly recovered Davies manuscript agrees with the Bodleian manuscript in the use of 'in such faith' (79), and though we cannot be certain when he made the alteration, Shelley enhanced rather than weakened the poem's coherence by changing the line to read 'But for such faith with nature reconciled'.[6] Reconciliation with nature implies an accord or identity with the phenomenal world that largely would nullify the metaphor of separate contributory streams with which the poem begins, the images of contending interchange by which it progresses and the concept of the mind's unique 'imaginings' with which it ends. The poem's two concluding sentences magnificently and comprehensively sum up its scope. From the opening imagery of things in relation to thought, through the observation of the actual material scene, to the symbolic representation of the out-of-sight snow fields, the poem leads to the conclusion that,

> The secret Strength of things
> Which governs thought, and to the infinite dome
> Of Heaven is as a law, inhabits thee!
> And what were thou, and earth, and stars, and sea,
> If to the human mind's imaginings
> Silence and solitude were vacancy?

> (139–44)

The commentary upon the mind's interrelationship with the phenomenal universe is still essentially that of the poem's opening passage, but with a heavier weight of emphasis on the ultimate responsibility that the mind has for the creation of meaning. The 'strength of things' governs thought only in the sense of setting certain limits upon the imagery available to the intellect. And this strength is declared to be 'as a law' to the 'infinite dome / Of Heaven' and also to 'inhabit' Mont Blanc, the mountain that symbolizes the continuum or collaboration of the material world of things with the realm of eternal essence.

In the interpretation of the poem's penultimate sentence, Shelley's phrasing of it in the Davies manuscript is enlightening. It reads:

> The secret strength of things
> Which governs thought, and to the infinite dome
> Of Heaven is as a column, rests on thee.

The function of phenomenal nature, including even the highest peak of Mont Blanc, is here clearly asserted to be that of providing a foundation and a pillar to support cognition, perception and imagination.[7] Thus the Davies manuscript version throws light on the poet's thinking with regard to the terms *law* and *inhabits* that are used in the version that Shelley published. The primary reason for not retaining the words *column* and *rests on* appears to be the avoidance of metaphorical images of solidity and stability that would clash with the images of fluidity and process that pervade the poem. The dome of Heaven, symbolizing the highest realms of thought and characterized by fast-alternating sunlight and cloud shadows, requires for its support or government not so much a column or foundation as a law for process. The association is with the law of Necessity (a concept early adopted by Shelley from Godwin) that is implicit in the processes of physical nature. As *column* and *rests on* in the Davies manuscript indicate, it is for Shelley a law of basis and support, rather than a regulating or defining code or dogma.[8]

The untitled sonnet in the notebook 'both renders and receives' clarity when juxtaposed not only with these concluding sentences but also with the opening passage of 'Mont Blanc'. As he does in the longer poem, the poet interacts with and learns from natural things:

[Sonnet I, Davies Manuscript]
Upon the wandering winds that thro' the sky
Will speed or slumber; on the waves of Ocean,
The forest depths that when the storm is nigh
Toss their grey pines with an inconstant motion,
The breath of evening that awakes no sound
But sends its spirit into all, the hush
Which, nurse of thought, old midnight pours around
A world whose pulse then beats not, o'er the gush
Of Dawn, & whate'er else is musical
My thoughts have swept until they have resigned
Like lutes inforced by the divinest thrall
Of some sweet lady's voice that which my mind
(Did not superior grace in others shown
Forbid such pride) would dream were all its own.

Having thought extensively on a wide range of natural phenomena – including winds, waves, forests, silent evening, the midnight hush and 'the gush/of dawn' – the poet concludes that he cannot lay full and absolute claim to *something* that he would like to believe totally the product of his own mind. The *something* which his thoughts have perforce 'resigned' appears to be the concept or notion of full autonomy, of creative power totally independent of basis and support in the sense-perceived world. The harmonized sound in his mind of the enumerated natural phenomena and 'whatever else is musical' is not to blame for the tonal quality of the lutes which, in the sonnet's lone simile, he likens to his own poetry in contrast to the 'sweet lady's voice', that is, others' poetry (very likely his new friend Byron's in particular). With a clear affinity to the 'organic Harps' and 'intellectual breeze' of Coleridge's 'Eolian Harp',[9] the sonnet gives positive assertion to a point that Coleridge's poem, by its retrogressive conclusion, demonstrates negatively: that the contribution made by the phenomena of nature to the individual mind depends upon the sensitivity or receptiveness of that mind. However intensely the poet's thoughts may have swept through the universe, the 'others', who give evidence of 'superior grace', have in his judgment given a response in some way superior to his own.

But the comparison with others is, after all, only parenthetically inserted. The important point is that nature does make its contribution, that the mind does not create in a vacuum. Indeed, external nature's contribution provides the standard by which the poet judges his voice to be not so graceful as the voices of others. Yet the sonnet constitutes a challenge for him to exert his mind even more energetically, now that it has rid itself of the delusion of sheer transcendence, to use well what nature offers. Again a comparison with Coleridge may be instructive. In 'Hymn before Sunrise' Coleridge, contemplating the various natural phenomena of Mont Blanc, recognizes that

> . . . like some sweet beguiling melody,
> So sweet, we know not we are listening to it,
> Thou, the meanwhile, wast blending with my Thought,
> Yea, with my Life and Life's own secret joy.
>
> (17–20)

In Coleridge this realization stirs the need to know the source and origin of so pervasive an influence. Searching all the natural manifestations of it, he finds them very deistically to 'Utter forth God' (69) as creator. Shelley's concern is more precisely intellect-focused. Not at all concerned with finding reassurance outside the self, he comes to realize (perhaps in part through the influence of Locke) that he must 'resign' the notion of the mind's complete autonomy and that the phenomena of nature must be given their due.

We should note, however, that the sonnet does not finally insist upon an equal sharing with nature; it asserts, rather, that the *something* that the mind of the poet has resigned is not 'all its own'. The implication is that it *may* be largely or mostly its own. There is an unmistakable parallelism between this conclusion and lines 5 and 6 of 'Mont Blanc':

> The source of human thought its tribute brings
> Of waters, – with a sound but half its own . . . .

That in the Davies manuscript version these two lines end with 'not all its own', and that the sonnet also deals with a contribution which the mind must admit is not 'all its own', may well indicate that (if any weighting at all is intended) the phrase 'but half' in the published version of 'Mont Blanc' means something like *nearly half* rather than *at least half*.

Suggesting the themes of Locke and also reminiscent of Wordsworth's emphasis in 'Tintern Abbey' on 'beauteous forms', there is a direct parallel between the predominant theme of 'Mont Blanc' and the sonnet's assertion (in its one inclusive sentence) that the things of nature do have a strength that governs thought, in the sense of providing a foundation and a column of support without which thought could not be structured. But the imagery, perhaps more clearly than that of 'Mont Blanc', suggests, instead of static support, an inhabiting law that buoys the poet's wide-ranging, sweeping thoughts so that they can sense the blending sounds and cadenced motions of all the speeding or resting winds, the waving ocean, the swaying tops of pines, the all-inspiring breath of evening, the poured-around hush of midnight and the gushing dawn. In the opening passage of 'Mont Blanc' there is the same concentration upon mutability and fluid motion. The difference is only that in the longer poem the 'universe of things / Flows through the mind', whereas in the sonnet the poet's 'thoughts have swept' upon and over the various aspects of the universe of things. What both poems assert is that, for creativity to occur, there must be the coming together – the flowing of the one over and/or into the other.

Instead of seeking in these poems to show, as Wordsworth had in *The Excursion*, 'How exquisitely the individual Mind / . . . to the external World/Is fitted: and how exquisitely, too –/. . . The external World is fitted to the Mind',[10] Shelley is concerned with the more Blakean question of which of them should predominate. The two poems approach the question from opposite perspectives. While the sonnet's informing assumption is that total autonomy of the mind is a proposition to be explored, the underlying principle in 'Mont Blanc' is the certainty that there is an irrevocable interaction between the mind and nature – all that which to it is *other*. And the tendencies of the two conclusions are against the operative assumptions of their respective poems, though more directly so in the sonnet than in 'Mont Blanc'. The sonnet's conclusion is, indeed, that the mind is not autonomous, thus bringing it into full accord with the principle around which 'Mont Blanc' is structured. The final sentence of the latter poem, however, suddenly though gently counters the tendency of its preceding emphasis by questioning whether, no matter how essential the world of things may be to thought, the human intellect does not after all hold a crucial predominance that has to do particularly with responsibly imaginative involvement.

> And what were thou, and earth, and stars, and sea,
> If to the human mind's imaginings
> Silence and solitude were vacancy?

This concluding rhetorical question suggests that meaning (the mind's contribution, without which there can be no human power) is, after all, the dominant stream in the confluence that gives rise to creativity or life. Upon the basis of meaning, of finding more than vacancy in even silence and solitude, the mind can choose and, in choosing, be creative.

Together, the notebook's opening sonnet and 'Mont Blanc' emphasize the awesome challenge to the creative human intellect to thread its way along the ledge of free choice that skirts the precipice of sense-perceived reality. They show that an adequate response to this challenge provides the only access to any experience of the glorious void of spiritual or imaginative potentiality – out of which in essence the universe is given form or created.

'Hymn to Intellectual Beauty', which just precedes 'Mont Blanc' in the Davies manuscript notebook, correlates well with the new sonnet 'To Laughter' to give unmistakable importance to the intangibility of that element in consciousness which in 'Mont Blanc' identifies true humanity. As lyric celebrations of the vital human resource in imagination which cannot be accounted for by means of empirical evidence or natural process, both 'To Laughter' and the 'Hymn' may be seen as works that test and find irrefutable the distinction between mind and things so important in the opening section of 'Mont Blanc'.

The very title 'Hymn to Intellectual Beauty' announces that Shelley considers the intellect to be the avenue through which whatever is good or beautiful becomes available to the individual. Being a direct address or prayer to the 'Spirit of Beauty' – 'some unseen Power' whose actuality is only intermittently made directly evident and is attested to at other times by the sensed presence of its inconstant and unseen shadow – the 'Hymn' emphasizes not only this power's apparent elusiveness (much like that of the sunlight, interspersed with cloud shadows, in 'Mont Blanc') but also the uniqueness of its knowledge-giving light. To underscore the elusiveness and uniqueness, the poet asks in stanza 2, 'Where art thou gone? / Why dost thou pass away . . . ?' and in stanza 3 asserts that the cults and creeds of humankind, symbolized by 'the name of God and ghosts and Heaven', have always been spells too weak to draw forth either a satisfactory explanation of these apparent absences or answers to related questions about the human condition.[11]

'Thy light alone,' the third stanza concludes, 'gives grace and truth to life's unquiet dream'. And this light shines not upon any special, spiritual intuitiveness but upon the mind's potentiality and upon real things perceived by the mind. The focus in both stanza 2 and stanza 4 is upon its effect on 'human thought'. It consecrates, the poet asserts, all that it shines upon 'of human thought or form' and (anticipating the opening of 'Mont Blanc') is nourishment to 'human thought'.[12]

Stanza 4, central in this seven-stanza poem, is designed to identify the unseen power. It opens with the assertion that

> Love, Hope, and Self-esteem, like clouds depart
> And come, for some uncertain moments lent.

That love, hope and self-esteem are not to be considered identical with Intellectual Beauty is clearly indicated by one word in the next sentence of the Davies manuscript. In the version that was published, the sentence reads:

> Man were immortal, and omnipotent,
> Didst thou, unknown and awful as thou art,
> Keep with thy glorious train firm state within
>   his heart.

> (39–41)

In this version, Intellectual Beauty (referred to by the pronoun *thou*) could be understood to be composed of 'Love, Hope, and Self-esteem'. The phrase 'thy glorious train' would then indicate an undefined or unidentified retinue of splendid, highly desirable qualities. However, the Davies manuscript, in which the pronoun *this* appears in place of *thy* in line 41, unmistakably designates the triad of 'Love, Hope, and Self-esteem' as constituting Intellectual Beauty's retinue of desirable human qualities, not as the components of Intellectual Beauty herself.[13] As the first line of the stanza asserts, these three human qualities are 'like clouds' that follow periods or patches of sunlight and thus constitute the sunlight's train. What would give immortality and omnipotence to mankind is not a remote other-worldly being, and not the removal of these glorious cloud-shadows that 'depart and come'. Rather, these grand qualities could be supplied by a 'firm state' of assurance within the human heart that the power behind love, hope and self-esteem is humanity's (or the individual's) own resource in mental integrity. Shelley's use, in lines 37–8, of the phrase 'depart/And come' (instead of the more ordinary 'come and go') may not be purely in response to the demands of rhyme; it may carry the suggestion that, like Intellectual Beauty or Wordsworth's 'natural piety', the qualities 'Love, Hope, and Self-esteem' are initially and originally inherent in human beings but that, like the light of Imagination in Wordsworth's 'Intimations' ode (75–6), they depart as the individual moves, darkling, into the 'light of common day' – that is, into rationalism or materialism.

In this regard the Davies manuscript also gives a clearer image in its version of the poem's first two lines. Instead of beginning,

> The awful shadow of some unseen Power
> Floats though unseen amongst us,

the Davies manuscript opens with,

> The lovely shadow of some awful Power
> Walks though unseen among us.

Although the double use of *unseen* in the published version
intensifies the emphasis on the intellectual essence of the power
by underscoring the logical impossibility of an unseen power's
casting a shadow which is then described as itself unseen, the
Davies manuscript version, with the exception of the word *walks*,
seems to me more pleasing and accurate in expressing Shelley's
intended thought. The Power (Intellectual Beauty), not its shadow,
is awful – in the sense of *awe-inspiring* – as line 40 also indicates.
The 'glorious shadow' (a composite of love, hope and self-esteem)[14]
is lovely, rather than awful, as it appears in the events of life. The
three qualities or powers of the shadow, when combined in a
simultaneous presence, are a tri-unity of the imaginative mind's
best, most desirable achievements in human society.

In this trinity, Love is first-named and apparently to be considered foremost, Hope is presented as the central or continuing
quality and Self-esteem is given the culminating position of commitment or personal involvement. As the poem's closing line makes
clear, Shelley does not mean by the third component any ego-
centredness or self-exaltation but, rather, the ability or willingness
of a person to 'fear himself' in the sense of the mind's providing a
proper regard or respect for one's own potentiality and human
responsibility. To be united with Love and Hope, this Self-esteem
requires, of course, a proper regard for the potentiality of all others
and thus obliges the individual to 'love all human kind'.

The seriousness of such socially imaginative self-respect is the
germ and theme of the second of the newly recovered Davies
manuscript sonnets:

> To Laughter
> Thy friends were never mine thou heartless
>   fiend:
> Silence and solitude & calm & storm,
> Hope, before whose veiled shrine all spirits bend
> In worship, & the rainbow vested form
> Of con[s]cience, that within thy hollow heart
> Can find no throne – the love of such great
>   powers
> Which has so requited mine in many hours

Of loneliness, thou ne'er hast felt; depart!
    Thou canst not bear the moon['] s great eye, thou
        fearest
A fair child clothed in smiles – aught that is high
    Or good or beautiful. – Thy voice is dearest
To those who mock at truth & Innocence[.]
I, now alone, weep without shame to see
    How many broken hearts lie bare to thee.

Though certainly it exaggerates (for Shelley often enjoyed laughter
and jesting), the sonnet is a powerful mood poem that directly
anticipates the thematic essence of the 'Hymn'. It is a poem about
that to which the poet has dedicated his highest abilities – about
the power behind and in 'Love, Hope, and Self-esteem'. Laughter
is obviously used in the restricted sense of derision, arrogance
and non-involvement. Though we have as evidence only the
juxtaposition of the poems in the manuscript notebook, Shelley
appears to be declaring to the world, before he begins the poem
which announces his disbelief in 'that false name with which our
youth is fed', that he does not mean to be classed as a proud,
sneering infidel – even though faith is replaced by self-esteem in
his trinity.

Conscience is, in line 5 of the sonnet, the term for self-esteem,
and (as in the 'Hymn') this important quality of the intellect is
linked with hope (line 3) and with love, which proceeds from
conscience and hope (line 6) and is imaged forth (lines 9–10) as
'the moon's great eye' and 'a fair child clothed in smiles'. But
'Silence and solitude' (the same concepts that in 'Mont Blanc' serve
as the test for the mind's self-reliance), as well as the natural
phenomena of calm and storm, are also declared to be qualities
that have won his friendship and love. With the charge that it is
the enemy of 'aught that is high / Or good or beautiful' and is the
favourite of 'those who mock at truth & Innocence', the poet
completes his case for laughter's being, indeed, the 'heartless fiend'
addressed in the poem's first line. The poet, by contrast, has spent
hours of loneliness, as he relates also in the 'Hymn', in a mentally
excruciating interchange of love with the powers that he enumer-
ates. And the sympathy expressed in the final couplet presents a
direct parallel to the love of 'all human kind' with which the
'Hymn' concludes. 'To Laughter' thus serves as an introductory

and companion poem to the 'Hymn' and also as a work importantly looking ahead to 'Mont Blanc'.

Not only has the discovery of the Scrope Davies manuscript notebook added two significant sonnets to the Shelley canon and clarified, by certain variants, portions of both 'Mont Blanc' and 'Hymn to Intellectual Beauty'; it has also given us these four poems in a grouping that demonstrates Shelley's remarkable mastery and consistency in handling both thematic material and poetic technique in 1816, at the youthful age of twenty-four. With this group of poems he gave evidence that *Alastor* had not been merely a fortuitous anomaly and established himself on the artistic plateau at which he created his greatest poetry – such as *Prometheus Unbound*, 'Ode to the West Wind' and *Adonais* – during the remaining six years of his life. Shelley's poetic powers remained dedicated to the theme of the challenge to the human intellect to recognize its own creative potential, not in some distant 'intense inane', but in the real world, where life's events or processes occur.

It is definitely in this world of actuality that Shelley, in 'Julian and Maddalo', explores and challenges the concept of the mind's responsibility and dominance, which are so strongly suggested in the earlier poems. Among Shelley's most poignantly presented victims of power-oriented and status-reliant systems is the Maniac of 'Julian and Maddalo'. Whatever else may have been involved in the Maniac's loss of sanity, he has been especially hurt, as Maddalo tells Julian,

> To hear but of the oppression of the strong,
> Or those absurd deceits . . .
> which carry through
> The excellent impostors of this Earth
> When they outface detection . . . .

> (239–43)

Strong in mind, he has not allowed the oppressors and sly impostors to outface *his* detection. Yet he seems not to have found a way to apply what he knows so as to transform the deceitful system of domination into the humane order that he obviously desires and needs. Particularly with regard to his opposition to deceit and oppression, Julian (explicitly an autobiographical character) acknowledges a close affinity between himself and the Maniac.

It is through the character of Julian that Shelley presents the possibility of coping with and overcoming the threat that the imaginative mind confronts in the form of systems as they are. Arguing against the more intimidated and fatalistic Maddalo's contention that human thoughts and desires are doomed always to transcend mortal attainment, Julian declares that our own will is at fault:

> '. . . It is our will
> That thus enchains us to permitted ill –
> We might be otherwise – we might be all
> We dream of happy, high, majestical.
> Where is the love, beauty and truth we seek
> But in our mind? and if we were not weak
> Should we be less in deed than in desire?'

(170–6)

To Maddalo's response that, since we *are* weak, such talk is utopian, Julian rejoins:

> '. . . Those who try may find
> How strong the chains are which our spirit bind;
> Brittle perchance as straw . . .
> We know
> That we have power over ourselves to do
> And suffer – what, we know not till we try'.

(180–6)

At this point Maddalo offers to introduce Julian to the Maniac in whom he sees a warning for spirits such as Julian's but whom, as Robinson has shown (94–8), Shelley intends as a composite figure representing a Byronic hero, fallen from the noble aspirations of Shelleyan visions and integrated with aspects drawn from Byron's *Lament of Tasso*. The two friends leave immediately for the island madhouse, where they find the Maniac and listen to his story. Though throughout this sad narrative there is a sense of danger that Julian may be drawn into the fate of the Maniac, he does survive spiritually as well as physically, as the Maniac does not.

Julian accepts personal responsibility as the primary challenge, and focuses on the intellect as the medium through which it is made functional. He does not declare that the will creates ill but, rather, that it permits us to be enchained by ill. Presumably, he would hold that even the Maniac could have been otherwise, that he could have used his strong mind to put into motion such influences in the real world that, whatever victimization might have been intended by his consort, he could have lived a sane and stimulating life in the knowledge that his was a current contrary to the force of ill. The assumption behind such a view must be, of course, that the strong-minded individual will not remain alone or isolated, but that others will be drawn to support the liberating cause.

That Julian, after visiting the Maniac, departs without alleviating his plight – that Maddalo, indeed, has done more in the way of tending to the Maniac's comfort – has seemed to critics an indication of Shelley's doubt regarding the ultimate efficacy of Julian's humane philosophy.[15] But such a concern seems beside the point, since Julian's aim and desire throughout the debate have been to show that the human will can create systems and conditions in which such ills as the Maniac's would be prevented. Robinson makes the point that, had Julian and Maddalo resumed their debate after visiting the Maniac, 'Julian could have claimed victory, for nowhere in the Maniac's history is there a cause and effect relation to substantiate Maddalo's contention that Shelleyan idealism, betrayed by destiny, leads to a "rent heart", frustrated "thoughts and . . . desires", and madness . . .' (101–2). Julian is convinced that, to substantiate or verify charitable acts, there must somehow be found a return to spiritual (mental) identification between and among individuals, so that the courage to test the will's power will not be lacking.

When, years later, Julian returns to Venice, obviously having resisted despair, and learns what has become of the Maniac, he elects not to divulge this information ('But the cold world shall not know'). Thus he throws out to the readers of the poem a challenge that, though perhaps a weak ending to the poem, yet contains the essential assertion that the intellect, if it is to know, must *will* to know. What the Maniac has failed to do and what Julian, by telling the story, hopes to accomplish is to keep intact the mind-to-mind chain of imaginative, humane involvement in the events of life and of the world.

No work of art has more concisely and convincingly portrayed than has Shelley's sonnet 'Ozymandias' both the method and the importance of keeping intact and extending this chain of imaginative identification through artistic expression. The message of the sonnet comes to the reader from far away and long ago, and it is relayed from traveller to author to reader. But the relaying of the inner message goes back far beyond the traveller who has seen the pedestal and the fallen statue in the desert. The characteristics of the shattered visage, half-sunken in the sand – a 'frown, / And wrinkled lip, and sneer of cold command' – have something to tell the traveller. What they tell him has to do not only with Ozymandias, whose statue this is, but also with the sculptor, whose art it is. Their message is that the sculptor 'well those passions read / Which yet survive, stamped on these lifeless things'. Since the traveller is convinced that the sculptor read the passions well, he is convinced also that Ozymandias was the frowning, scowling, sneering, aloof commander that the statue portrays him to have been.

As the traveller clearly notes, it is the half-buried face of the fallen statue that tells that the sculptor so well read (interpreted) the passions which (because the sculptor has put them skilfully into the lifeless stone) survive both the artist, whose hand 'mocked [copied]' them, and Ozymandias himself, whose heart 'fed' them. The traveller is convinced that this was a skilful sculptor who, through the art object that he has created continues to tell the truth about a man of power. Having seen the inscription on the pedestal,

> 'My name is Ozymandias, King of Kings,
> Look on my works, ye Mighty, and despair!'

which is the written form of what the sculptor has portrayed in the statue, the traveller is able to convey a sense of Ozymandias's proud certainty that all must despair of equalling him in the accomplishments of power. We cannot be certain that the traveller understands the irony that he himself throws upon this proud certainty by his own concluding observation:

Nothing beside remains. Round the decay
Of that colossal Wreck, boundless and bare
The lone and level sands stretch far away.

Nor need we know with absolute certainty that the poet understands the irony (though who, knowing Shelley, can doubt that
he understands it?). All these artists – the sculptor, the traveller
(whose telling is art) and the poet – have told only what they saw
or heard – clearly, without embellishment, without commentary –
and have yet conveyed the ironic truth that Ozymandias was a
fool for not seeing that all systems based on power, wealth and
glory are doomed to despair.

An even more important message they convey is that the
involved, imaginative artist can indeed prevail ultimately. But the
ability to prevail depends upon the quality of the art – its ability to
inspire – and upon the capacity of the reader, viewer or hearer to
respond to the message of the art. That response, be it the creation
or re-creation of an art form or an involvement directly in the
events of life, constitutes the enduring quality of art. Jean Hall (21–
2) expresses this concept in terms of the image's being transformed
as it passes from person to person. Metaphorically, she presents
the successive contexts of 'Ozymandias' as a set of nesting Chinese
boxes, with the implication of an ever-enlarging context for the
central box or focus.

Not necessarily achieving early recognition or eliciting an immediate response, true art may thus be a long, perhaps endless, time
achieving its ends. We do not know whether the sculptor's
prophetic insight raised the thoughts and stirred the actions of any
of his fellow-citizens. Perhaps it did; it may even have had
something to do with the decline of Ozymandias's system. We
do know, however, that the sculptor's involved, and therefore
commendable, reading of life has outlasted the power of Ozymandias and continues to inspire thoughts and actions that suggest
alternatives to such power systems.

The Cenci is another work in which Shelley suggests that, if the
mind would but exert its imaginative potential, the subjection to
systems of power and calculation could be broken. Admittedly, in
all five acts of its dramatic progression, *The Cenci* intensifies the
impression that the system that is first represented by Count Cenci
and, after his murder, by the Papal Court is invincible in its

disregard of the individual and in its ponderous obstruction of all living process. Betrayed by the self-serving Orsino and ineffectively served by the well-intentioned but system-bound Cardinal Camillo, Beatrice Cenci, in desperation, takes the situation into her own hands and directs the murder of her father. Primarily for this stepping outside the convention of paternal despotism, the Pope and Court reject all pleas that, on the grounds of having suffered intolerable oppression, Beatrice be pardoned; they condemn her to death. As he states in the drama's dedication to Leigh Hunt, Shelley saw this historically-based drama as 'a sad reality', as 'that which has been' (237). In this world of actual events it does appear that Beatrice has been cornered, all escape routes being effectively barred. Shelley, with high artistic integrity, much as does the traveller in 'Ozymandias', tells what he has seen; that is, he relates in his drama what he has found in his manuscript source for the Cenci story.

In the Preface, however, he explains clearly that he thinks Beatrice had available a way of action that she did not take. It is the way of total risk on the side of life. In accord with what Julian, in 'Julian and Maddalo', says of the power of the will, Shelley asserts,

> Undoubtedly, no person can be truly dishonoured by the act of another; and the fit return to make to the most enormous injuries is kindness and forbearance, and a resolution to convert the injurer from his dark passions by peace and love. Revenge, retaliation, atonement, are pernicious mistakes. If Beatrice had thought in this manner she would have been wiser and better.
>
> (240)

Immediately, though, he points out that had Beatrice acted thus, she could not have been a tragic character, not because of any disharmony with the potentiality of life, but because the artistic form would not permit it; conventional views of the art of tragedy would preclude the necessary imaginative identification: 'The few whom such an exhibition would have interested, could never have been sufficiently interested for a dramatic purpose, from the want of finding sympathy in their interest among the mass who surround them' (240).

It is contrary to Shelley's concept of mind and individual responsibility to say as does James D. Wilson (81–2) that, straight after she is raped, 'Beatrice becomes an unwilling vessel for the spirit of absolute evil. Subsequently possessed by the devil, she can only let the spirit exorcise itself by destroying its progenitor.'[16] This is, of course the majority view, the view of the mass of people who, not having the requisite confidence in the creative potentiality of thought, consider the individual subject to irresistible forces and see violence as the only recourse when such forces take over. Aware of this prevailing point of view, Shelley presents the 'sad reality' of Beatrice's situation in the context of a world that imagines no alternatives. Nowhere does he imply that an alternative would be easy to find or to practice; the drama demonstrates only that Beatrice does not find or elect the alternative which Shelley's Preface declares to be possible. For Shelley the question of art's relation to life remains a vital concern; having determined to keep pressing his art as close to actual life as is possible, he adopts the conventional point of view to show what a moral entrapment it can become.

That he depends on *The Cenci* to challenge the audience to serious thought, and through it to an alteration in their actions, is revealed in his next assertion:

> It is in the restless and anatomizing casuistry with which men seek the justification of Beatrice, yet feel that she has done what needs justification; it is in the superstitious horror with which they contemplate alike her wrongs and their revenge; that the dramatic character of what she did and suffered, consists. (240)

Stuart Curran (*Shelley's Cenci*, 133) correctly says of the problem that confronts Beatrice: 'To impose one's will upon the formless savagery of an irrational world is an absolute imperative, but any such act can precipitate a cataclysm.' What needs to be added is that, in Shelley's view, this is the case only because people have allowed this 'sad reality' to develop. In the world that *could* be, imposing one's will would not denote retaliation or violent action; it can mean an inexhaustibly imaginative, peaceful, loving strategy.

Shelley hopes that people who see or read the play will recognize that they cannot avoid personal responsibility for changing their own system, which is essentially like the one in which Beatrice confronts her tragedy. Beatrice is driven to such a point of desperation that conventionally-minded persons cannot avoid attributing justice to her act of parricide while simultaneously finding no way to deny the justice of her being punished for this very act. It is up to the individual members of the audience to determine what they will do when in their minds they have recognized their responsibility.[17] Shelley believes that, just as the chain of imaginative continuity in 'Ozymandias' will help people to act in a loving rather than despotic manner, so the audience's or reader's thinking about what Beatrice Cenci could or should have done will ultimately have an effect on the apparently invincible system.

'The Cloud' and 'To a Skylark' are two poems in which Shelley demonstrates both the mind's exultation in the ability to accept process as the basis of life and also its sense of deprivation at not achieving full involvement in this process. In its vaporous insubstantiality, presented as more essentially process than matter, the cloud can and does glory and luxuriate in its condition of continually becoming, yet never attaining. The skylark, similarly, is in essence a process of sound that is going on, floating and soaring, all around the narrator but is not bodily present in the sense of being visible. In point of view lies the essential difference between the two poems. Personified as the speaker of its poem, the cloud lets the reader see, from an imagined experiential perspective, what it is like to find oneself identified with process – to be the very personification of it.[18] In 'To a Skylark', however, the speaker is a person who, because of his physical condition, is not able to see the world from the perspective of the 'blithe Spirit', yet imagines it like the speaker of 'Ode to the West Wind' and achieves an identification with the spirit of change and becoming.

Continually shifting from metaphor to simile to personification, from one metric mode to another and from one quick rhyme to another, the poem 'The Cloud' itself constitutes an aesthetic imitation of an ever-changing cloud. Having, in the first two stanzas, taken the reader through an experience of the various atmospheric conditions occasioned by different interactions of air and water (constituents of a cloud), and having then let the reader experience in stanzas three and four the different successive times of day from its higher perspective, the cloud as narrator uses images of power and effectiveness in stanza five to expound on its relationship with vast and pervasive phenomena of the universe:

I bind the Sun's throne with a burning zone
   And the Moon's with a girdle of pearl;
The volcanoes are dim and the stars reel and swim
   When the whirlwinds my banner unfurl.
From cape to cape, with a bridge-like shape,
   Over a torrent sea,
Sunbeam-proof, I hang like a roof –
   The mountains its columns be!
The triumphal arch, through which I march
   With hurricane, fire, and snow,
When the Powers of the Air, are chained to my
     chair,
   Is the million-coloured Bow;
The sphere-fire above its soft colours wove
   While the moist Earth was laughing below.

(59–72)

The images of power and domination used here include binding
the thrones of both sun and moon, dimming the glow of volcanoes,
setting stars reeling, bridging the sea and covering it as does a
roof. Served by whirlwind, hurricane, fire and snow – the 'Powers
of the Air' – the cloud can use the rainbow as its triumphal arch,
to demonstrate to the happy earth that in process there is to be
found the true strength of the universe.

But the poem does not end in this exultation in power; instead,
the narration shifts drastically in the final stanza to identify the
cloud with images of the 'daughter', the 'nurseling' and the process
of osmosis. Declaring, 'I change, but I cannot die' (76), the cloud
accepts self-annihilation in the form of the 'blue dome of the Air'
(80) which is the 'cenotaph' or commemorative marker of the
cloud's having passed away. However, because the cloud's essence
is not so much material substance as it is process itself, its passing
does not mean its death. As its transition into annihilation has
been the building of the blue-sky cenotaph, so its return appearance
in a new form is the unbuilding of that cenotaph.

Thus the images of strength and domination used in stanza five
are shown not to represent physical, materialistic conquest but,
rather, the subtly pervasive power that is latent and potential in
the human intellect, the power to accept one's true strength, that
of being in the organic process of becoming, not of gaining

materialistic domination. The cloud, indeed, is a power in the universe, but it comes into its power through its essential love of the universe. This love is actually the ability of the cloud to abandon its separate identity in order to do its part in the universal process by becoming small or diffused enough to pass through minute 'pores, of ocean and shores' (75) to an apparently total annihilation – only to arrive at a newly refined being with vast potentiality. Then it can again march triumphantly through its arch, straddle the sea and bind the thrones of sun and moon. At the end of the poem, we see clearly that these are actions of involvement and participation rather than of domination and exploitation. This is the way the human mind must learn to operate, Shelley is saying, if it is to find power that is not illusory.

The narrator of 'To a Skylark', as he tries to imagine what the bird is or what is most like it, also uses figures of speech that emphasize transitoriness and uncalculating outpourings of beauty and thought. At the head of his list of similies is the thought-encompassed poet:

> Like a Poet hidden
> In the light of thought,
> Singing hymns unbidden,
> Till the world is wrought
> To sympathy with hopes and fears it heeded not.
>
> (36–40)

The poet's singing is unbidden because his or her ego is not evident or predominant; the self is hidden in thought that reaches out to the world and, through sympathetic involvement, changes the world's focus of attention.

The 'hymns unbidden' have an affinity with 'that serene and blessed mood', in Wordsworth's 'Tintern Abbey', in which,

> . . . with an eye made quiet by the power
> Of harmony, and the deep power of joy,
> We see into the life of things.
>
> (47–9)

They also relate closely to the essential question in Coleridge's 'Eolian Harp':

> And what if all of animated nature
> Be but organic Harps diversely fram'd,
> That tremble into thought, as o'er them sweeps
> Plastic and vast, one intellectual breeze,
> At once the soul of each, and God of all?

(44-8)

Based also in part (though not without Shelley's own attitude of challenging it) on Hume's concept of the known universe as composed only of our uncaused ideas in succession, which in turn has links with Locke's questioning of the human mind's powers, Shelley's poet, 'hidden in the light of thought', is not isolated or impotent in this hidden state but, rather, is in a position effectively though unobtrusively to gain the world's attention. Like this thought-immersed poet and the images of self-giving contributors in the succeeding similes (41–60), the skylark's music 'doth surpass' (60). The skylark pours itself forth in a non-calculating process of becoming sound instead of substance and thus changes the world of the narrator for the better.[19]

Having realized that this is the value of the bird for him, the narrator wants human beings to make a similar contribution and again emphasizes thought as the key ingredient in the process that might enable them to do so.

> Teach us, Sprite or Bird,
> What sweet thoughts are thine.

(61–2)

Yet, though he has likened the skylark's song to that of the thought-involved poet, he deplores the seeming incapacity of people, poets presumably included, to attain the joyousness of thought of which the bird must be capable.[20] His lament is that 'Our sweetest songs are those that tell of saddest thought' (90). Teaching, learning, knowing, brain action – these are the concepts involved in his desire to attain the bird's free indulgence in joy:

> Teach me half the gladness
> That thy brain must know.

(101–2)

And the consummate aim of this intellectual comprehension of joy is that 'The world should listen then – as I am listening now' (105).

Like the cloud, the skylark has a joy that is inherent in its organic oneness with the universe in which it exists. Without mental reservation or self-conscious calculation, both the cloud and the skylark can and do throw themselves into that existence and thus become much more than their separate, material, substantive beings could ever be. In an important though subtle way, the cloud and skylark symbolize the mind's role in 'Mont Blanc' and 'Hymn to Intellectual Beauty'. The cloud, by its presence or absence, becomes the determiner of the atmosphere enveloping the earth, and the skylark, by its outpouring of song, becomes a sky-filling process of inspiring sound that constitutes the narrator's affective environment. To Shelley it appears that what these two representations of nature do because it is natural to them, people should be able to do, in their own way, because their brains are capable of willing freely and of directing what their individual actions or contributions are to be.

3

The Emphasis on Love

Shelley's belief in the human mind's responsibility to know and to build upon the things of nature is, as we have seen, unmistakably evident. That this responsibility is not merely a facet of the human condition, without basis or specific origin, has already several times been suggested. And in Shelley's view the ground of the mind's necessity to interact with natural things is love. Intellectual pursuits separated from love, he holds, are isolating as well as destructive endeavours – just as love separated from intellect is vapid sentimentality or else mere passion. To fulfil its ultimate purpose, then, thought must manifest itself in love, as also, conversely, to be a potent force in life, love must be the embodiment and culminating form of thought.

As in the essay 'On Life' he has defined life in terms of a universal mind of which each individual mind forms a unit or element, so in the brief essay 'On Love' Shelley defines love as the urge toward union or community with another, with others or with all that is not self. Love, he says, 'is that powerful attraction towards all that we conceive or fear or hope beyond ourselves when we find within our own thoughts the chasm of an insufficient void and seek to awaken in all things that are, a community with what we experience within ourselves' (473). The emphasis throughout the essay is on sharing with another being or with other beings something of value to the self, not at all on securing something for the self or on satisfying the ego. In total consistency with his emphasis on mind as the creator of reality and value, he presents both the void chasm and the love that can bridge it as entities within the mind.

One may imagine that Shelley was contemplating the theme of 'On Love' as he composed a stanza of *The Revolt of Islam* that is particularly concerned with the mind's creative process. Having just related how greatly he had in youth desired that humanity might be roused from its ages-long swoon as with a burst of 'cleansing fire', Laon, in Canto 2, tells how the creative process

worked in his mind to awaken in others a community with what
he had experienced within himself:

> These hopes found words through which my spirit sought
> To weave a bondage of such sympathy,
> As might create some response to the thought
> Which ruled me now – and as the vapours lie
> Bright in the outspread morning's radiancy,
> So were these thoughts invested with the light
> Of language: and all bosoms made reply
> On which its lustre streamed, whene'er it might
> Through darkness wide and deep those tranced spirits smite.[1]

It is Laon's own spirit, not any extrinsic power or influence, that
makes use of words to bring about the human sympathy that
creates responsive thought in others. Language, a product of
the mind, provides the necessary light for the actualization or
germination of thoughts. There is a close parallel with Asia's report
in *Prometheus Unbound* of Prometheus' gift of the power of language:

> He gave man speech, and speech created thought,
> Which is the measure of the universe.

> (2.4.72–3)

William Keach suggests that this poetic assertion may be at least
in part based on Locke's view in Book 3 of the *Essay Concerning
Human Understanding* that knowledge has 'so near a connexion
with words, that unless their force and manner of Signification
were first well observed, there could be very little said clearly and
pertinently concerning Knowledge'. As Keach explains, although
names (words) are for Locke the work of the mind, they are in
turn the material that makes the mind's work possible (37). The
thought that matters to Shelley is that which can 'measure the
universe', which can comprehend and identify with what is beyond
self-interest – in other words, which can love – and he sees
language as clearly antecedent to such thought.

The creative, imaginatively-identifying use of language, then, is
the quintessential act of love, of sharing one's original and genuine
ideas with others. To communicate avidly and honestly the truth
that one sees is in essence to express love, to bring to the other

that which is of true value to the self. Shelley's art always brings us round to a direct confrontation of what it means really to live – which for him is synonymous with really to love. The relatively early poem *Alastor* (1815) comprehensively illustrates this point.

Before exploring the poem itself, we must understand the title and Shelley's Preface as well as their linked relationship to what is in the poem. The term 'alastor', suggested by Thomas Love Peacock when Shelley was at a loss for a title, means a pursuing, avenging spirit;[2] and the sub-title 'The Spirit of Solitude' indicates that Shelley thought of separateness or alienation as the spirit that operates in such vengefully pursuing manner in the poem. Many readers have found difficulty in understanding how pursuit by this spirit can be said to be the theme when the action of the poem centres almost exclusively on the Poet himself (who, notice, is unnamed) as the pursuer of a vision. The Preface (69–70) is helpful in this regard.

Shelley makes explicit in the Preface that this is a poem about the human mind. The main character, the youthful Poet, may then be said to represent a searching mind. Having for a while indulged himself joyously in seeking knowledge wherever it could be found, this youthful Poet becomes dissatisfied with what he has learned and is suddenly awakened to his need for a oneness with the most perfect 'Being' that he can imagine or 'depicture'. Accepting a single image or vision as the ideal of this Being, he seeks for a realization of it but soon perishes in his unsuccessful quest. So much for the first paragraph of Shelley's Preface; the important, clarifying point comes in the second paragraph.

There is an easily misconstrued concept in this paragraph's second sentence: 'The Poet's self-centred seclusion was avenged by the furies of an irresistible passion pursuing him to speedy ruin.' The destructive force is not in the 'irresistible passion' itself. This power would not strike the poet (one of the world's 'luminaries') with 'darkness and extinction' – would not be 'too exquisite a perception' for him – if his spirit had been vitalized instead of being kept in its vacancy by the conditioning influence of his having grown up 'among those who attempt to exist without human sympathy'. And those so designated are the 'unforeseeing multitudes' of the earth; they are the vast majority, the ones in control as well as the masses who are controlled; they are the materialistic crowd, doomed to a 'slow and poisonous decay' precisely because they have never accepted the 'domination' of the impulsive power that overwhelms the young Poet of *Alastor*.

The situation and fate of the Poet, even in the mistaken quest to which he is driven, is unquestionably preferable to that of these dull, rationalistic, unfeeling materialists. He has at least responded to an original impulse from within him. It is unfortunate that he has not earlier detected and counteracted the conditioning of his unresisting spirit toward vacancy and self-centred isolation, a conditioning that has been foisted on him by a kind of unthinking but massive social pressure. Had he detected and obliterated within himself the propensity toward unloving, isolated existence, his sudden new awareness would have been simply his great awakening to the potentialities for human, imaginative identification all about him. Or, better still, had the masses who have constituted his social environment long ago seen and been rightly guided by the light that the Poet suddenly sees, he would not have been alienated or isolated in the first place, but would have been very differently conditioned in a society of love that seems to us all but unimaginable. It is something like this that Shelley means to convey to us before we begin the reading of the poem itself.

Alastor begins with a 49-line invocation and ends with a 49-line conclusion. An important feature of both passages is the image of an alchemist earnestly working with fire to achieve a vital transformation (29–37, 681–6). From beginning to end, the poem is concerned with the elements of being and particularly with the element that incorporates the potentiality to transform life from emptiness to fulfilment – the element of love, of which fire is the cogent symbol.

Invoking not only the maternal power of nature, but more specifically the favour of the 'beloved brotherhood' earth, ocean, and air, the narrator immediately emphasizes Shelley's theme and the narrator's own primary concern in the poem. The 'beloved brethern' readily bring to mind the classical concept of the four elements of the universe – one, namely fire, not being addressed. Instead of including the element associated with love as a brother of the other three, the narrator bases his appeal for the favour of the three 'brethern' on the evidences that love has gone forth *from him* to all things in nature. As fire is more specific in its source and range of effectuality, not a pervasive element as are the other three, so love has its source in the individual and exerts its effect as it emanates from the individual. Also appealing for the favour of the 'Mother of this unfathomable world' – the maternal power of nature – the narrator declares that he himself has avidly persisted in love. The invocation serves, then, to establish love as the element of human consciousness that is different from all others in that it is not given from without but must be supplied from within.

The other three elements are those that form the essential images in 'Mont Blanc': the earthen ravine, the gushing waters of the streams of things and of mental sources, and the airy spaces of all around and about the narrator and the mountain. 'Mont Blanc' concludes with an emphasis on the human mind's airy ability to soar and to imagine the farthest recesses of the mountain world of earth and water. Whatever of fire imagery there is in the poem is presented in the remote forms of sun and lightning. The focus in *Alastor*, however, is on the need for the fire element to be supplied by the conscious, individual self. More closely related to the element of air than to earth and water, fire (or love) may be said to be in league with air (or mind) to constitute the world of the human spirit, as contrasted with earth (matter) and water (material or natural process), the elements of the physical world. The four elements basically symbolizing completeness or unity of being, the narrator recognizes that, as artist representing the highest function of the human mind, he must supply or creatively infuse that fourth element toward completion – the fire of love.[3]

Without the illuminating, warming, welding power of love's fire, the mind's airy domination remains in the realms of silence and solitude and the other two brethern are not brought into any potential for an active, living society of human advancement. The invocation ends, indeed, with the narrator's declaring to Nature:

> I wait thy breath, Great Parent, that my strain
> May modulate with murmurs of the air,
> And motions of the forests and the sea,
> And voice of living beings, and woven hymns
> Of night and day, and the deep heart of man.
>
> (45–9)

Somehow, in the course of nature's exhalations, this contribution from the self, this flame of fire, depending for its source upon the narrator himself,[4] needs to become the catalytic element of blending among earth, ocean (water) and air – and, by extension, among the lives, arts and consciousness of human beings.

The narrative begins with the announcement of the decline and desolate death of the youthful Poet, the main character whose story the narrator tells and whose death he laments. In giving, at the outset, the gist of his dismal tale, the narrator employs two important terms from the final line of 'Mont Blanc': *solitude* (60) and *silence* (65). In both poems they are terms which must have focal meaning, must impart understanding. But in *Alastor* they apply to more than the vast natural and intellectual spaces symbolized by the mountain's remotest peaks; they apply to 'the deep heart of man' that weaves its 'hymns/Of night and day' and from which must well the 'voice of living beings' – an interesting and illuminating interpretation of Wordsworth's 'language really used by men'. If the human heart is characterized by solitude and the human voice by silence, it must be because of a vacancy caused by a missing element that needs to be discovered, as in 'Mont Blanc', by the 'human mind's imaginings'.

The imagery of the four elements suggests that what is missing in the *Alastor* Poet is the fire of love. The narrator, being (as we have seen) the representative and advocate of this fourth element, tells the tale from the perspective of the missing or inoperative element that could have provided joyous attainment and meaning to the life of the Poet. The narrator knows what needs to enter into the vacancy in the Poet's heart if the Poet is to represent anything more than a cold, unknown and unvisited peak of Mont Blanc.

In a passage from *A Defence of Poetry* quoted in this book's introductory chapter, Shelley says of love that it is 'an identification of ourselves with the beautiful which exists in thought, action, or person, not our own'; of imagination he says that it is a putting of oneself 'in the place of another'. Thus Shelley declares love and imagination to be in effect united, as Asia and Prometheus ideally are united. The phrase 'the human mind's imaginings' in 'Mont Blanc', however, is to be taken on a more abstractly philosophical plane, as relating to the mind's ability to deal creatively with the phenomena of nature or of necessary processes, thus to remove from them the aspect of vacancy. Not that this imaginative love of nature could not include human beings if they were present in the scene; the emphasis in 'Mont Blanc', though, is on the functioning of the mind rather than on the interpersonal love that the mind can generate. It seems that, having written *Alastor*, Shelley went back in 'Mont Blanc' to identify the underpinnings for the earlier poem's revelation about the mind and love.

To love another human being is to carry further the principle of the mind's responsibility. It is to enter into the other's condition or perspective on the world, to imagine that person in the sense of creating oneself with his or her image of reality. The object is to gain that proper regard ('fear') of oneself as one also gains the love for humankind that Shelley prays for in the last line of 'Hymn to Intellectual Beauty'. To do so, the mind must accept love as its method, must be united with (in that sense, wedded to) love, thus expelling solitude and silence, replacing them with imaginative union and creative expression.

In the early narrative paragraphs of *Alastor* the Poet cultivates in himself the imagination to deal creatively with the elements of nature – and that is highly commendable – but does not develop human love. The climactic occurrence in the poem, an explicit opportunity for the Poet's enlightenment, is presented in lines 149 to 191. The Poet's visionary dream of a veiled maiden represents to him all that his own soul regards as beauty and truth. The dream vision represents art. Highly erotic in the most noble sense of the term, it permits the poet an experience of imaginative union with the veiled maiden. This union becomes the ideal of all his subsequent waking hours, an ideal that drives him relentlessly throughout his futile quest for a re-attainment of what he believes to be the reality of union. The extent of the difference that this dream experience makes in the Poet's life is emphasized in the assertion that, on the following morning,

> His wan eyes
> Gaze on the empty scene as vacantly
> As ocean's moon looks on the moon in heaven.

> (200–2)

In other words, all the details and particulars of the material universe that have absorbed his interest in the past now appear to him so unreal that they can best be described by the image of the reflection of a reflection (as the moon's reflected light being not only reflected in the ocean but also reflected back upon the moon).[5] The Poet mistakes art for life.

The reflection image looks ahead to the Poet's pursuit, through-

out the remainder of the narrative, of reflected or apparently
mentally mirrored points of light that ultimately, in the death
scene, consummate in another image of the moon's reflected light.
Immediately after using the startling simile of the vacancy in the
ocean's reflection of the reflecting moon, Shelley presents us with
an assertion, upon our interpretation of which depends our
understanding of the avenging alastor that pursues the Poet to an
untimely death. The assertion is:

> The spirit of sweet human love has sent
> A vision to the sleep of him who spurned
> Her choicest gifts.

> (203–5)

It does not seem likely that 'the spirit of sweet human love' would
be vengeful or destructive in its response to the human failure of
the Poet. The vision, then, can scarcely be considered the alastor.
Rather, the vision has been sent as the next-best 'gift' or the
second-chance opportunity for the Poet to find the true unity that
he needs.

What, then, have been the 'choicest gifts' that the Poet has
'spurned'? In the poetic paragraph just preceding the one which
tells of the vision, they have been imaged for us:

> Meanwhile an Arab maiden brought his food,
> Her daily portion, from her father's tent,
> And spread her matting for his couch, and stole
> From duties and repose to tend his steps: –
> Enamoured, yet not daring to for deep awe
> To speak her love: – and watched his nightly sleep,
> Sleepless herself, to gaze upon his lips
> Parted in slumber, whence the regular breath
> Of innocent dreams arose: then, when red morn
> Made paler the pale moon, to her cold home
> Wildered, and wan, and panting, she returned.

> (129–39)

The Arab maiden is *in* the real world that is so negatively presented
in Shelley's Preface, but she is not *of* it. Indeed, in a loving,

imaginative response to her the Poet could find all that is necessary to fill the (to quote from the Preface) 'vacancy of [his] spirit' that 'suddenly makes itself felt'. The Arab maiden identifies absolutely with him and visits him, not as an intruder but as the very embodiment of Intellectual Beauty, as a 'messenger of sympathies' whose power of love is offered freely but remains inert unless there is a response in kind from the intended recipient of that offering. Not yet having sensed the vacancy of his spirit, because he has not received from the past, from his entire societal milieu or from his own consciousness, any sense of genuine imaginative identification with others, the Poet totally disregards the Arab maiden's offer of an opportunity for a fulfilment in love, in actual human responsiveness.

Subsequently, the Poet misses the second-chance opportunity offered by the vision, the opportunity to find his way back by means of aesthetic awareness to the truth offered by the Arab maiden. Having spurned the 'choicest gifts' of the 'spirit of sweet human love', he responds to the vision in a manner quite contrary to its purpose. Instead of learning from it that he must become aware of and responsive to the potentiality of human love, he eagerly pursues 'beyond the realms of dream' – that is, in real life – not the substance but the 'fleeting shade' of love. In his response to his artistic perception, he 'overleaps the bounds' (207), assuming that reattainment of or perpetual association with the artistic, aesthetically sensed vision is enough. By misinterpreting the vision as an end or entity in itself, the Poet tragically fails to grasp its import.

Translated into ordinary experience, this drastic misinterpretation of the vision means misunderstanding and misusing art (imaginative expression) as a realm withdrawn from life instead of accepting it for what it is: a vehicle to bring us to where life really is.[6] What the Poet, after all, needs is a meaningful contact with humanity. But humanity is not *in* the vision; life is not *in* art. The vision, if it is to accomplish its mission, must lead him to humanity. We know that he has had at least one opportunity for a human experience to which he could have related fully: the Arab maiden episode. And the vision comes to remind him that it is not too late to take advantage of that kind of opportunity. The Poet's rapid decline and early death result not from the fact of his having had the vision but from the way in which he responds to it. Despite his aesthetic sensitivity and intense idealism, he does not break out of self-centred seclusion.

The pursuit of the vision seems in fact to dull and harden the Poet to human approaches. Among the masses there are those 'cottagers' who minister 'with human charity / His human wants', and there are their daughters, the 'youthful maidens' who call him 'brother' and 'friend' but see him go unresponsively on his way (254–71). All indications are that it is not the vision but his unwillingness or inability to comprehend its true import that leads to his rapid decline and ruin. In essence, he expects too much from it. For there is no other truth that we can know as we know the truth in life, in the living of it. Though the vision (art, aesthetic beauty, imaginative perception, spiritual intuition) could guide the Poet to an awareness of the opportunities for and in life, he finds it more attractive to lose himself in the art object or in the abstract aesthetic ideal itself than to go the way that it points out.

Pursuing the vision, the Poet is led into a kind of unreal existence, imaged in the poem by his miraculously crossing the ocean in a disintegrating boat, the boat's gravity-defying ascent up a spiraling mountain current and the vision's partial and mysterious reappearances in reflected and apparent twin-light forms. This surrealistic pattern culminates in the Poet's unnaturally rapid ageing and physical decline, which bring him soon to his not unwelcome death. The silent nook in which he finally attains release, though it is in the very heart of nature, is entirely removed from humanity:

> One step,
> One human step alone, has ever broken
> The stillness of its solitude.

(589–90)

This death in absolute estrangement from human contact – past, present and future – is in the most profound sense unreal, for it is entirely outside the scope of involvement with the real, intellectual, loving processes of living.

It appears that the Poet never recognizes the vision as only a reflecting transmitter of light and that he also does not see or acknowledge anything unifying, whole or of meaning in life – of which the vision tells. His continuing delusion is symbolized in the death scene by the setting moon. The crescent moon, mostly hidden behind the almost vertical mountainside, still reveals its two points of light, still reflects for him (though now revealed to him only as disconnected spots of light) the true light from the original source which he, alas, has not seen and apparently does not, even in death, understand. Still displaying the quality of responding to the light that he has – the quality for which Shelley praises him in the Preface – the Poet keeps his dying eyes focused on the specks of reflected light that remain until the moon has set. He appears never to realize that his gaze is averted from the true light that he seeks.

The true source of the light that is reflected by the moon to the dying Poet is the life-giving sun. As the ultimate source of fire and light, the sun serves well to symbolize the ability to love that the Poet has really though subconsciously been seeking. The ineffectuality of art without this love active in life is graphically expressed by the narrator in the concluding passage of the poem:

> Art and eloquence,
> And all the shows o' the world are frail and vain
> To weep a loss that turns their lights to shade.
> It is a woe too 'deep for tears,' when all
> Is reft at once, when some surpassing Spirit,
> Whose light adorned the world around it, leaves
> Those who remain behind, not sobs or groans,
> The passionate tumult of a clinging hope;
> But pale despair and cold tranquility,
> Nature's vast frame, the web of human things,
> Birth and the grave, that are not as they were.

When life (in which only can love exist) is lost, the very lights of art (reflections of the love that is in life) are naturally turned to shade. The young Poet who has just died has been a 'surpassing Spirit' in that, compared to 'the world around', he has had a light that he was willing to follow, even though it was only a reflection. After his death, nature, human things, death and the grave 'are not as they were' because while he lived they were at least contexts within which he, as a conscious human being, could have found a way to love.[7] Though, as in the Conclusion of 'The Sensitive Plant', the truth or eternity of things remains as it always was, the great difference is that the potentiality of the Poet's finding its real implications no longer exists. The narrator's voice, of course primary in the concluding lament, underscores this vacancy by expressing the 'pale despair' of unfulfilled possibility that he so strongly feels because of the Poet's death. Now fully to assume the role of poet, the narrator needs to accept himself as the living perpetuator of the element of love's fire that, as artist, he in essence is. He needs to take instruction and do otherwise than the young protagonist of the poem has done. In one sense things are 'not as they were' because, now that he has before him the whole episode, including the dismal result of an artist's life isolated from human involvement, the narrator, as the voice of love, has the challenge of finding a way of infusing into creative instances of the future a consciousness in artists as well as audiences that art and life are inseparable.

The narrator seems aware that if the Poet had turned to trace the trail of the reflected light back and forth to its source, he would have found the true light to originate in human love. Genuine art gives evidence that love does exist; it finds its consummation in leading people to an experience of love.

That the Poet has engaged in the quest, though mistakenly, is to his high credit; it has kept him within the range of the light of love. Missing in the development of his mind, however, has been the element of the fire of love, which could have warmed his awareness; he lacks the capacity to respond to the aura of love that identifies another. Had he realized that he was pursuing a reflection and that reflections essentially give evidence of sources, he could have taken direction from it and would then have found his way back to what the Arab maiden represents. The reality of her challenging him to love gives rise to the vision, whose sole purpose is to lead him back to the truth represented in the real-life maiden: that self-annihilating identification with another or with others is the love which is the light of life.

Other poems attest also to Shelley's belief that love can, and indeed must for human survival, be found in people's daily lives rather than in an abstract world of unrealizable fantasy. In 'Lines Written Among the Euganean Hills', telling of a traveller who anticipates arrival at 'the haven of the grave', he asks,

> What, if there no friends will greet;
> What, if there no heart will meet
> His with love's impatient beat;

> Wander wheresoe'er he may,
> Can he dream before that day
> To find refuge from distress
> In friendship's smile, in love's caress?

(27–33)

And the response is that if this kind of loving relationship is found in earthly life, then all questions about consolation or attainment in any state of being beyond the grave become unimportant:

> Then 'twill wreak him little woe
> Whether such there be or no.

(34–5)

Although the poem is occasioned by Shelley's despondency over the lack of such an atmosphere of love in the society he knows, the narrator works his way through to the conclusion that it can or could be made experiential.

For Shelley the narrator's metaphorical arrival that morning at the island of the inspirational moment is a culmination of a process that has left in its wake the skull and seven dry bones of the past (45–65), a culmination that parallels in microcosm history's arrival at the present moment, leaving behind a sinking Venice and an obsolescent Padua. On the small island in the first rays of the morning sun, the narrator sees some high-flying rooks as they emerge from the early mists that have given them a gray appearance. Reflecting sparkles and glints of sunlight, they become in his sight a multi-coloured splendour that, while not erasing the narrator's awareness of the scientific fact that rooks are but black birds, makes them in that moment far more real in his eyes and mind as a process of sun-reflecting beauty. Of primary importance in this passage is what the mind perceives and, as Shelley emphasizes in the essay 'On Life', the mind's ability to order what it perceives. Thus the poem, both actually and symbolically, presents the integration of the imaginative and the actual. What we observe as we read is a response to the living truth of the moment as it unfolds. To deny the reality and beauty of the sparkles and glints would be as absurd as to deny the fact that rooks are black birds.

Likewise, as the sun's rays touch the towers and spires of Venice, the narrator sees that the city, despite its history of decline, may yet be valued for the island of humanity's blossoming that it has been and for the beauty and goodness that it has nurtured and preserved in harbouring great art and true artists. The human mind, like Venice, can accept poetic truth for what it is and can preserve it, even though it may be figurative truth in the world at large.

Throughout the day the narrator, exploring what is revealed in the light of the sun, imagines scenes, one of which is of the historically renowned city of learning, Padua (visible, like Venice, from the Euganean Hills), as a burnt-out lamp whose now-departed light is burning and shining elsewhere. As in a similar image in the later 'Ode to the West Wind', the mind's sparks can be scattered and perpetuated to form new fiery islands of joyfully expanding freedom and discovery such as Padua once was.

Finally the process of his mind's explorations brings the narrator back to self-awareness and the realization that the islands, on one of which he has spent time that day, are not merely passing moments of respite from the voyage but are the permanent realities to which the boat can be securely moored, much as the garden of 'The Sensitive Plant' is an eternally self-renewing constant in a world in which *self* – as contrasted with the essence of the universe around it – is continually altering. And what may become of these islands when the light of creative imagination shines on them is as high in potentiality as has been the flight of the rooks into the morning sunlight. Why not, then, go to one of these islands with his freedom-loving friends and build there a process of life that can function in accord with imaginative potentiality not to be perverted by even the arrival of the 'polluting multitude' (356)? 'They, not it, would change' (370), says the narrator. The way to go there is for the mind to accept the potentiality that such isles have for realization and to work toward that end.

For Shelley these islands of solid actuality, when imaginative involvement becomes their atmosphere, not only make possible but are themselves indeed the love, beauty and delight of which he speaks in the Conclusion of 'The Sensitive Plant', where, after having described winter's horrid effect upon the once-beautiful garden, he declares:

> That garden sweet, that lady fair
> And all sweet shapes and odours there

In truth have never past away –
'Tis we, 'tis ours, are changed – not they.

For love, and beauty, and delight
There is no death nor change: their might
Exceeds our organs – which endure
No light – being themselves obscure.

(130–7)

In other words, the possibility for the experiencing of love, beauty
and delight is not prevented by nature, by any fate inherent in the
real world; but it may be, and virtually always is, prevented by
our own flowing with the tide of appearances. In declaring that
"tis we, 'tis ours, are changed', Shelley is asserting simply that we
do not have the needed steadfastness in applying the means of
love, a resource which is always there for us. The appearance is
that love is weak and that it fades; in reality, love's potentiality is
constant, but weak people fade in resolve.

   In 'Euganean Hills' Shelley has directed our course clearly and
consistently to the conclusion that the process of history, honestly
studied and responded to, leads to a distinct focus on one's own
genuine perception – to be followed, of course, by action consistent
therewith. And in a kind of apparent irony, true personal perception leads to casting off the historically accumulated selfhood or
self-interest and simultaneously to a thoughtful recognition that
others, too, may have and may wish to exercise this new, free
selfhood. Unlike the young Poet of *Alastor*, who in his drive for
self-satisfaction fails to break through to this awareness, the
narrator of 'Euganean Hills' recognizes clearly that it is only in the
love of all humankind that a freed selfhood has any meaning.

Shelley's most emphatic expression of the urgency and effect of
such outgoing love occurs in 'Ode to the West Wind', a stirring,
vibrant poem that takes up where 'Hymn to Intellectual Beauty'
leaves off. The impulse to join the process of imaginatively creative
involvement with humankind carries through from the opening
exclamation of adoration, 'O wild West Wind, thou breath of
Autumn's being', to the concluding rhetorical question that signifies
achieved, assenting involvement: 'O Wind, / If Winter comes, can
Spring be far behind?'

The autumn Wind, that in its observed action appears to be ripping and flinging life away, is in actuality cooperating creatively with its 'sister of the Spring' to bring about new life. The speaker of the poem effectively applies to this robustly affective wind the terms 'Destroyer and Preserver'. As the ode progresses, it makes increasingly apparent that what needs both destroying and preserving is the conscious selfhood of the speaker. He needs not only to be transmuted by the wind as are the leaves, clouds and waves in the successive stanzas 1, 2 and 3; he needs, also and more importantly, to become the agent of that transition.[8] In other words, if he does not destroy his assumed selfhood so that its place can be taken by the Wind, so that the Wind itself can be his very self, he will be unable to move and transform what, symbolically represented, are the leaves, clouds and waves of effective involvement in the world of social, human progress and improvement. Wind, being itself in essence the atmosphere, may be said to create itself, since changes in atmospheric conditions create the currents of air that constitute wind. Becoming actively moving wind, the atmosphere destroys what it has been: inactively still air. But it is only through this self-destructive creation of its own new self that the wind can exude creativity in the world of trees and sky and sea. The imagery of this self-destroying creativeness is entirely fitting for what the ode's speaker must learn and must accomplish.

After describing, in the first three stanzas, the action of this simultaneously counter-directional force that creates, uncreates and recreates itself, the speaker expresses in the final two stanzas his intense desire to identify with it – to experience, to be and to do what it experiences, is and does. The often-misinterpreted (and therefore disparaged) line, 'I fall upon the thorns of life! I bleed!' (54), is an expression of his frustration over being so limited in his physical and psychological existence that he seemingly cannot enter totally into the wind's full involvement, in all processes in which it participates.[9] The speaker laments the fact that he cannot simultaneously retain conscious involvement and be physically annihilated – that physical life precludes the creation of a self of totally identifying essence which could, in turn, lose itself in finding the wind's power to destroy what is old while creating what is to be. This is a paradoxical dilemma closely akin to or identical with the self-esteem that means 'to fear himself and love all human kind'. The speaker needs that proper awe of, or regard for, himself that would enable him to exert the power of self to uncreate its old form in order to merge with the expansive new form of life-infusing creative identification.

Only by turning his desires around, by vacating his selfhood to the point of imploring,

> Be thou, Spirit fierce,
> My spirit! Be thou me, impetuous one!

> (61–2)

can he hope to achieve the true self-esteem that has an effect on human society, to be 'The trumpet of a prophecy!' The selfhood that he destroys is, after all, only that which bars or hinders full involvement with the formative events that essentially constitute life itself. Achieving identity with the Wind by means of persuading it to assume or usurp his very self, the speaker becomes himself that 'breath of Autumn's being' which he addresses with awe in the ode's first line. His physical body is the material instrument, but the Wind is the trumpet call, and that is from within him; it is his true essence. It is he himself.[10]

The West Wind being the very essence or spirit of the transitional event known as autumn, the speaker's attainment of its self makes *him* the spirit of the event of change.[11] To give oneself so fully to the cause of life is for Shelley the essence of love. The 'ashes and sparks' that are to be scattered by him, from the 'unextinguished hearth' of his identifying imagination, to humankind (66–7) give evidence that, unlike the *Alastor* Poet, he has indeed realized within himself the all-important element of love's fire. As it tragically fails to do in *Alastor*, the fire of love in 'Ode to the West Wind' rightfully performs its role as the element that culminates and gives fulfilment to the interactions and unitings of the other three elements – the air or wind of mental potentiality, the earth of matter, and the water of material or natural process. The speaker of the ode has demonstrated how a person may achieve the ability to 'fear himself and love all human kind'.

The Wind having ultimately taken on the poet's selfhood or identity, the ode's final question,

> O Wind,
> If Winter comes, can Spring be far behind?

presents the speaker as really addressing to his own truest self the challenge to continue as the courageously involved 'Destroyer and Preserver' who dares to interact with life wherever he moves. Then the process symbolized by the coming springtime will not be blocked. The poem is about the achievement of a genuine, imaginatively involved, creative selfhood that is not afraid to act for changes in society.

In a more playful tone and manner, Shelley presents in 'The Witch of Atlas' the embodiment of such an involved, identifying selfhood. A daughter of the sun-god Apollo, the Witch is repeatedly likened to and identified with love. In first describing her delightful attributes, Shelley tells us that 'her low voice was heard like love, and drew / All living things towards this wonder new' (87–8), and that when her fellow nymphs and nature-gods are sceptical of her qualities, 'Her love subdued their wonder and their mirth' (128). Neither gods nor humans can resist the Witch's attractiveness,

> For she was beautiful – her beauty made
>   The bright world dim, and every thing beside
> Seemed like the fleeting image of a shade:
>   No thought of living spirit could abide –
> Which to her looks had ever been betrayed,
>   On any object in the world so wide,
> On any hope within the circling skies,
>   But on her form, and in her inmost eyes.

(137–44)

Aware of her beauty's power to distract thought from all the appearances of life, she weaves for herself a veil, which Shelley significantly describes as 'A shadow for the splendour of her love' (152). Thus we are given to understand that her beauty consists of her love, that it is because she loves that she is beautiful. And it is this attractive love that has such power over living beings that it must somehow be veiled so as not to distract people's thoughts from the necessary attention to objects 'in the world so wide' in which they live.

In the recesses of the cave which is her dwelling, the Witch has 'Visions', pent up cocoon-like to be released at her behest when the right time arrives (161–8). The imagery is reminiscent of the

West Wind's power to preserve for its sister of the spring the potentialities for new life and growth. Even more closely parallel to the imagery of 'Ode to the West Wind' is that of the next stanza:

> And odours in a kind of aviary
>   Of ever blooming Eden-trees she kept . . .
>   . . . and each was an adept,
> When loosed and missioned, making wings of winds,
> To stir sweet thoughts or sad, in destined minds.

(169–76)

A few stanzas later, we learn that

>   . . . Her own thoughts were each a minister,
>   Clothing themselves or with the Ocean foam,
>   Or with the wind, or with the speed of fire,
>   To work whatever purposes might come
>   Into her mind.

(210–14)

Thus, in her power over the loving impulses which themselves constitute her essential being, the Witch is seen to be a kind of spiritual personification of the West Wind.

The poem is, indeed, loaded with imagery of 'wintry winds' (282), 'autumn leaves' (287), 'clouds . . . / The bastions of the storm' (430–1), and 'lake beneath the lash / Of the wind's scourge' (441–2).[12] But through it all there is the pervasive emphasis upon the underlying, transforming power of the Witch's love, which is ultimately in full command of whatever situations arise. By means of her light, magical boat (almost itself a leaf wafted by the wind), she navigates the elements wherever her will directs. When she indulges in 'her choice sport' (497) of 'observing mortals in their sleep' (528), she moves 'With motion like the spirit of that wind / Whose soft step deepens slumber' (521–2). As she moves in and among the minds of the sleepers, the Witch beholds each as a living spirit, and though we are told that she does not yet know what sexual love is (584–6), the more all-encompassing love that constitutes her being is evident in her ability to 'make that Spirit mingle with her own' (576).

In her essay on this poem, Andelys Wood, citing Perkins and

Grabo for support, concludes that Shelley treats the 'capricious' Witch irreverently and that the poem

> marks the beginning of Shelley's realization that poetry is not only inadequate to express pure thought, but is false and deceiving because it distorts the thought in the attempt. It is a playful poem, but the ironies underlying the frivolity express Shelley's weakening poetic faith. (82)

But we need not conclude that Shelley, because he uses a comical, light-heartedly satiric tone (essentially to counter Wordsworth's plodding 'realism' in *Peter Bell*), is directing the satire against his own ideal of thoughtful mind-challenging poetry. What he presents as frivolity is intended, rather, as an indication of the felicity with which changes in human affairs might be achieved if the social mind-set were actually, as is the Witch, the creation of love. The parallel to be drawn is with Julian's declaration in 'Julian and Maddalo':

> . . . Those who try may find
> How strong the chains are which our spirit bind;
> Brittle perchance as straw. . . . We are assured
> Much may be conquered, much may be endured
> Of what degrades and crushes us. We know
> That we have power over ourselves to do
> And suffer – what, we know not till we try.

> (180–6)

As Shelley asserts at the conclusion of 'To Mary', his light-hearted dedication to 'The Witch of Atlas', to unveil the Witch is to discover love that becomes idolatry – scarcely a note that suggests any weakening of poetic faith.

It is in the mingling of human spirits with her own that the Witch becomes aware not only of human pleasures and contentments but also of the distortions in human thinking that bring about 'the strife / Which stirs the liquid surface of man's life' (543–4). As personification of all that is beautifully loving, she cannot tolerate these distortions and goes to work in people's minds to set them aright – sending into them the stored 'Visions' referred to earlier, here playfully called 'pranks' (665) – to bring about a new springtime of human thought, much as will the buried seeds and the unextinguished sparks of 'Ode to the West Wind'.

If 'The Witch of Atlas' seems a poem easily misunderstood or one whose images and implications are hard to comprehend with assurance, there is certainly no relief from difficult complications as the reader takes up the study of 'Epipsychidion'. Shelley himself was keenly aware of the obstacles to this poem's being made comprehensible, as is evident not only in his correspondence about it but also in portions of the poem itself. Not far into the poem, he pauses to exclaim:

> Ah, woe is me!
> What have I dared? where am I lifted? how
> Shall I descend, and perish not? I know
> That Love makes all things equal: I have heard
> By my own heart this joyous truth averred:
> The spirit of the worm beneath the sod
> In love and worship, blends itself with God.

(123–9)

Contained in the artistic frustration voiced in these lines are both a sense of despair regarding the efficacy of words to fit the intended meaning and a forthright declaration of the poem's intended theme. The sense of semantic despair is not strong enough to cause the poet to abandon the project; it serves, rather, as a moment of reassurance that the flaw is not in his art or dedication but in the inadequacy of his tools. More important for the reader is the blunt expostulation of thematic intent that accompanies the frustration with words. The difficult task that he has begun, says the poet, is the attempt to express in words his heart-felt certainty that to love is to become one with, in a full sense to identify with, all things. In the act of loving (here equated with the act of worshipping) one is no more inspired or awed by God than by the spirit or essence of life in a worm. How to present this essential definition of love and not find his poem crumbling under the weight of it is his concern in this interruption as well as at the poem's conclusion, where he similarly laments,

> Woe is me!
> The winged words on which my soul would pierce

Into the height of love's rare Universe,
Are chains of lead around its flight of fire –
I pant, I sink, I tremble, I expire!

(587–91)

And his concern has, over the years, proven not unfounded. There has been much more critical involvement in the identification of autobiographical relationships represented by various figures or images in the poem than in the perception of their metaphorical significance. Shelley means these images to convey an understanding of the tremendous mental challenge and great responsibility that he finds in an acceptance of love in its proper role. But the concern with the biographical correspondences of the symbolic figures meant for this purpose has tended to deflect attention from the many attempts in the poem to clarify the meaning of love and to point out its vital attributes.[13]

Most prominent among these attributes is the essential unity of those who love. Early in the poem, the narrator declares to Emily that he is 'not thine: I am part of *thee*' (52), and attempting to account for the beautiful warmth of Emily's being, he attributes it to the

. . . unentangled intermixture, made
By Love, of light and motion: one intense
Diffusion, one serene Omnipresence . . .

(93–5)

In the concluding portion of the poem, in which he envisions an elopement to an ideal place or condition, the narrator proposes their indulgence in this unifying love to the point at which the whole sense of otherness will disappear:

Possessing and possest by all that is
Within that calm circumference of bliss,
And by each other, till to love and live
Be one.

(549–52)

And this desire that they might lose – and simultaneously find –
themselves in each other intensifies as the narrator continues his
declaration of what he envisions:

> We shall become the same, we shall be one
> Spirit within two frames, oh! wherefore two?
> One passion in twin-hearts, which grows and grew,
> 'Till like two meteors of expanding flame,
> Those spheres instinct with it become the same.

> (573–7)

Finally the apex of the vision, as also the crescendo of his verbal
effort, is reached as the narrator desires that he and Emily become

> One hope within two wills, one will beneath
> Two overshadowing minds, one life, one death,
> One Heaven, one Hell, one immortality,
> And one annihilation.

> (584–7)

The higher his aspirations rise and the more he strains and taxes
his vocabulary, the more the imagery is associated with concepts
of the human mind, of intellectual attainment. Love and its unity
are thus again shown to be functions and responsibilities of the
individual and collective human mind. There is a very down-to-
earth logic involved in the perception that in unity with others,
not in isolation from them, there is the fulfilment of desire and
joy.

The same logically imaginative perception leads to the poem's
elucidation of a second highly important attribute of love: its
essential indivisibility, even as it is dispersed.

> True Love in this differs from gold and clay,
> That to divide is not to take away.
> Love is like understanding, that grows bright,
> Gazing on many truths; 'tis like thy light,
> Imagination! which from earth and sky,
> And from the depths of human phantasy,
> As from a thousand prisms and mirrors, fills

The Universe with glorious beams, and kills
Error, the worm, with many a sun-like arrow
Of its reverberated lightning.

(160–9)

The same is true, says the narrator, of pleasure and thought (180); these three mental excellences thus differ radically from the more material, unpleasant phenomena of 'suffering and dross', which may be diminished and eventually even 'consumed away' by repeated division (178–9). It is in this kind of living multipliability that the strength of love resides. It is this that makes it stronger even than death,

Who rides upon a thought, and makes his way
Through temple, tower, and palace, and the array
Of arms: more strength has Love than he or they.

(402–4)

Presented as an entity conveyed by thought, death is here interestingly contrasted with love, whose association with thought has already been emphasized. The mind that activates the principle of non-diminishable love is thus clearly and logically seen as the living mind – as contrasted with the dying mind that relies upon the destructible, diminishable materials represented by the images of temple, tower, palace and arms.

The third of those qualities attributed to love in 'Epipsychidion', closely related to its essential unity and undiminishability, is the quality of process or becoming, of being subject to no limits. Emily is described as

. . . a mortal shape indued
With love and life and light and deity,
And motion which may change but cannot die . . .
a tender
Reflection of the eternal Moon of Love
Under whose motions life's dull billows move.

(112–9)

The emphasis is upon her adaptability and variety as well as upon the eternally reliable and responsible process of the love that is her energy and light. She is as creatively adaptable and as undying as is the cloud in Shelley's poem of that name. Later, describing Emily's entrance into his life, the narrator compares her to 'an Incarnation of the Sun, / When light is changed to love' (335–6), the important characteristics again being the connection between light and love and the transmutability of the former into the latter. Process, mutability and potentiality for new growth are the attributes that the narrator focuses on as he addresses the 'Twin Spheres of light who rule this passive Earth, / This world of love, this *me*' (345–6), asking them to 'Govern [his] sphere of being' (361)

> And, through the shadow of the seasons three,
> From Spring to Autumn's sere maturity,
> Light it into the Winter of the tomb,
> Where it may ripen to a brighter bloom.

> (364–7)

A similar image of the end of a period of time is used as the narrator addresses the Comet – another giver and object of love – asking that it become for him 'love's folding-star' (374). But these images of the passing of life need not be taken to refer to physical death. They seem, rather, to lead up to love's bringing about for the lovers, in this new-found unity, a dying into each other, thus creating for them a new life or being. The addressing of the lines to three different imaged individuals identifies this attribute of love also with the attribute of love's undiminishability. The upshot or ultimate realization of true love, because it has the qualities of unity, undiminishability and process, is its imparting to people the essence of liberty: 'It overleaps all fence' (398).

But at this point the linguistic limitation rears its head in the poem as in our commentary upon it, and that is what Shelley laments at several points in the poem. He knows that images of the overleaping of fences and of elopement carry connotations of irresponsibility, escapism and even criminality – connotations that he does not at all intend to convey and that stand directly in the way of what he wants people to see about love. Realizing this inherent weakness of language, he, in the envoy, commands his 'Weak Verses' to haste to the hearts of individual persons

And bid them love each other and be blest:
And leave the troop which errs, and which reproves,
And come and be my guest, – for I am Love's.

This conclusion is akin to that of *Alastor*, in which the narrator of that poem finds that 'Art and eloquence, / . . . are frail and vain / To weep a loss that turns their lights to shade' (710–12), that images made by the materials of art (words, in the case of poetry) cannot convey the essence of love, of life. Shelley expresses the concept best perhaps in *Prometheus Unbound*, in the assertion that 'the deep truth is imageless' (2.4.116), that if love's deep truth is to be expressed, it must find that expression in life itself, for the images of art cannot express what it really is. The envoy of 'Epipsychidion' asks quite simply that people do with love what art after all cannot do with it – that they *live* it.

In *Adonais*, his elegy on the death of John Keats, Shelley, with mythological support, presents love, which in 'Epipsychidion' has been shown to be undiminishable, as the only life that has a claim upon eternity. The death of so promising a young genius as Keats appears to compel Shelley to confront the essential importance of the individual's (and especially the artist's) mind-oriented, imaginative involvement in life, in maintaining a loving communion and continuity with the lives and well-being of others.

This involvement in life carries with it the unavoidable risk of being misinterpreted and (what is more personally devastating) of actually wrongful action – both of which entail retaliation at the hands of society. Shelley makes the point in his presentation of the apparently autobiographically-related poet in *Adonais*, who

> . . . with a sudden hand
> Made bare his branded and ensanguined brow,
> Which was like Cain's or Christ's – Oh! that it should
> be so!

> (304–6)

As Shelley himself explained in a letter to his Irish friend John Taffe, 'the introduction of the name of *Christ* as an antithesis to *Cain* is surely any thing but irreverence or sarcasm' (*Letters*, 2.306). The names of Christ and Cain, as Webb emphasizes (167), are not interchangeable but are to be taken as symbolizing a clear-cut contrast between murderous Cain's suffering at the hands of the orthodox – 'unpardonable in those who caused it, but in one sense justifiable' – and Christ's suffering: the suffering of humanity's harmless benefactor. Both Cain and Christ have acted in society – Cain's action being an involvement in death-dealing hate, Christ's an involvement in life-enhancing love.

Though Shelley's intent is clearly that poets be on the side of love, he realizes that the results of involvement even with the best intention and most careful consideration, cannot be fully known in advance and that, even if the results are beneficial, their interpretation by an orthodox society may be cruelly judgmental. The Cain-or-Christ imagery, then, encompasses the risk that the poets' intended Christ-like involvement may eventuate in its Cain-like opposite as well as the likelihood that, like Christ's, the poets' successful adherence to their true purpose will result in scorn and suffering being heaped upon them by society. As the poet in *Adonais* makes bare his brow, he symbolically reveals the recrimination that (not unlike the pain that the critics had inflicted on Keats) Shelley himself has suffered for his involvement in the condition of humanity. By implication, since the poem ends by celebrating the immortality attained by Adonais, Shelley may hope that in the eye of eternity his own commitment will gain the reward that he knows Keats's has attained. Keats, having vitally and lovingly confronted life, has left for Shelley the reassuring evidence of a working process of immortality which perpetually renews as the art that he has created continues to confront the issues of life.

Love and *life* become, in the course of the vital confrontation in *Adonais*, contending opposites. The term *love* comes to designate the true way of living: *life* takes on the connotation of the deceptive, anti-love way of existence in materialistic society. A creative reinterpretation of the Adonis myth of regenerative life, *Adonais* provides not only a worthy tribute to Keats and clear evidence that Shelley knew the soul of Keats's poetry, but also an artistic disclosure of the point to which Shelley's spiritual quest ultimately led him.

In the final one-third of the poem, Shelley achieves the consumate expression of what his own mature life has focused upon and what is simultaneously the essential point of identity between himself and Keats: the primacy and the permanence of human thought (Perkins, 131–3), especially regarding the concept of immortality, which both poets perceive as the ability of love to transcend death. Having employed the Adonis myth to sympathize with and celebrate Keats in largely traditional elegaic form throughout the first two-thirds of the poem, Shelley changes pace in the final nineteen stanzas. In this final section of the poem the narrator's essential assumption of philosophical conviction is in full accord with what Keats suggests and articulates in much of his poetry, most specificially in the powerful near-epic *Hyperion* as well as in the sonnet 'When I Have Fears': that life, love and immortality are all attributes of and have meaning only in the domain of human thought.

Hyperion (the poem used by Shelley in several letters[14] to give Byron evidence of Keats's poetic quality) makes use of the myth of the fall of the Titans particularly to emphasize the omnipotence and the consequent responsibility of human thought. In Book 3, when the decline and fall of the gods has been thoroughly accounted for, the poem presents the transformation of Apollo from the merely mortal condition to the state of godhead, in which he is ready to replace the doomed Hyperion. The transformation, excruciatingly difficult and self-annihilating, is entirely a process of thought. The goddess Mnemosyne does not give Apollo an answer to his question, 'Where is power?' He must read the lesson in her silent face. And he comes to know in his own mind that:

> Knowledge enormous makes a God of me.
> Names, deeds, grey legends, dire events, rebellions,
> Majesties, sovran voices, agonies,
> Creations and destroyings all at once
> Pour into the wide hollows of my brain,
> And deify me . . .[15]

Apollo realizes that any genuinely creative power that he can have must originate in his mind, through intellectual involvement in any and all aspects of the human condition, and cannot be brought about by an escape from such involvements through aesthetic indulgence, such as his wandering on a remote isle 'Full ankle-deep in lillies of the vale' (3.35) and his having produced a 'tuneful wonder' by touching the strings of his golden lyre. Apollo's new strength comes through his love for people – through the enormous knowledge of the events that constitute their lives – a love that is attained by a process of thought. It involves a death to the indulgent self-gratification that by general consensus is normally defined as *life* or *living*. Only by responsible identification in and with the realm of thought does Apollo attain the immortality that depends upon his ministering to the needs of people, in both a particualr and a universal sense.

In the sonnet 'When I have Fears' Keats condenses the Apollo-deification process into fourteen lines and through the use of the personal pronoun *I* brings it home more directly to the individual. The poet's fears have to do with his future non-existence, with all the self-realization that will no longer be his when he no longer is. In line 7 he uses the term *think* in the sense of self-interested stream-of-consciousness calculation: 'And think that I may never live to trace / Their shadows . . .'. This thought has to do with his own potential for fame. He then (line 9) uses the term *feel* to express his sense of being deprived of his 'relish in the faery power / Of unreflecting love'. Though the term *unreflecting* may take on a note of irony in its suggestion of Narcissus – whose fate is relevant to what then seemed likely for the poems of both Keats and Shelley – it seems in the sonnet to be synonymous with *thoughtless* or *sensate*. And this self-indulgent love sinks with the self-consciousness of fame to nothingness when the poet can 'stand alone' 'on the shore / Of the wide world' and 'think'. This time the word *think* connotes a use of the full range of mental powers. He does not stand ankle-deep in lilies on a remote isle but on the shore of the wide world, in touch with human experience. The knowledge enormous that he thus attains is the power by which his dread sense of mortality is annihilated. Full, deep involvement in the realities of humanity produces the absence in the mind of fretful concern about mortality.

Returning to the final one-third of Shelley's *Adonais*, we find that it celebrates precisely this achievement of immortality and concludes with the poet's own Apollo-like transition to the state of immortality in the realm of thought.[16] The elegy thus serves to underline a most vital point in Keats's poetry as well as to identify it with Shelley's own spiritual aspiration and progression.

The poem opens with the assertion that Adonais is dead: an assertion directly contradicted in stanza 39 by the declaration that 'he is not dead . . . / He hath awakened from the dream of life' (333–4). In subsequent stanzas we read that 'He has outsoared the shadow of our night . . .'; 'He lives, he wakes'; 'He is a presence to be felt and known . . . / Spreading itself where'er that Power may move / Which has withdrawn his being to its own'. The 'Power' with which Adonais has become united is clearly the power of human thought. In stanza 43 Shelley calls it 'the one Spirit's plastic stress' and characterizes it as giving form to – that is, making comprehensible – the 'new successions' in the evolving material world. It is in the last half of stanza 44 that we find articulated the essential philosophy of the poem and indeed the essence of Shelley's spiritually mature belief about mortality and immortality.

> When lofty thought
> Lifts a young heart above its mortal lair,
> And love and life contend in it, for what
> Shall be its earthly doom, the dead live there
> And move like winds of light on dark and stormy air.

The important and truly memorable moments, Shelley is saying, are the moments in the realm of human thought when the legacy of prior human thought affects crucial decisions.

That the contending forces in the realm of thought should be love and life may at first seem confusing, both terms being usually considered positive or pleasant. We need to remember, however, that in stanza 39 conventional life is defined negatively as 'the dream of life' in which 'we, . . . lost in stormy vision, keep / With phantoms an unprofitable strife, / And in mad trance, strike with our spirit's knife / Invulnerable nothings'.[17] Here Shelley seems to deal ironically with the difference between reality and the paradise of dream that Scrivener (275) sees as a concept relating this poem to 'Ode to a Nightingale'. Keats's ode declares that in the realm of reality, 'but to think is to be full of sorrow / And leaden-eyed despairs'.

In *Adonais*, as Scrivener (276) points out, it is Misery who in the earlier portion of the poem (stanza 22) calls upon Urania to awaken. In that episode the misery consists in the special, mournful occasion of Adonais's death; in stanza 39, however, misery in the form of 'stormy visions', 'phantoms' and 'unprofitable strife' is pervasive in the 'dream of life' that has come to be seen in the poem as all that 'reality' really is.[18] Were Misery at this point to address Urania, it would be not to awaken her but to invite her to sleep, so that she could be present to observe, and perhaps awaken people from, the false dream called *life*.

'Paradise', says Scrivener, 'exists in *Adonais*, unlike utopia in *Prometheus Unbound*, as a limited potentiality, coexisting with a dominant actuality which is the very negation of paradise' (275). If, then, the notion of paradise as dream has been distorted and negated by the dream's succumbing to the nightmare of actuality, the real paradise must lie elsewhere. And Shelley designates its sphere as that of genuine mental engagement and productivity, which he has come to see as the only actuality. This is the same interpretation of life that Shelley presents in his final, fragmentary poem 'The Triumph of Life', in which all but 'the sacred few' are victimized by a blind, frenzied force that bears the name of life.

In stanza 44 of *Adonais* this deceptiveness (which is usually called life) struggles in the young, deciding heart against love (which is the human identification inherent in the 'knowledge enormous' experienced by Keats's Apollo). The outcome of this struggle determines the young individual's 'doom' (we would say *destiny*) in his or her mortal existence. It is in these moments of decision that 'the dead live'; the thoughts they have expressed when alive can make the all-important difference in the destiny of the young person who must decide. This, says Shelley, is the eternal life to which Adonais has awakened. As Anthony Knerr explains, 'The creative minds of the dead are a living influence on "a young heart"' (96n). *Adonais*, then, is really more an ode to Keats's artistic life than an elegy on his physical death. The influence that his thought has had and will have in the multitudes of such decisions of destiny is immortality enough.

As the elegy has made amply clear, the legacy of thought that Adonais has left is emphatically on the side of love. Had it been on the side of what is conventionally called life, it would not be immortality at all, for it would then lead to the 'mad trance' in which the participants encounter those horrid-appearing forces which are in reality the deceptively challenging 'invulnerable nothings'.

In stanza 47 Shelley challenges the reader to indulge the mind in a contemplation by means of which he or she can know both self and Adonais correctly. The direction given the reader for the gaining of such knowledge is:

> Clasp with thy panting soul the pendulous Earth;
> As from a centre, dart thy spirit's light
> Beyond all worlds, until its spacious might

Satiate the void circumference: then shrink
Even to a point within our day and night.

For Shelley, the 'spacious might' of the human 'spirit's light', by
which he means the light of human thought, is that power which
essentially creates the universe, from the most grandly spacious
to the most minutely contracted of its aspects. And when this
might is exerted upon a study of death (stanzas 48–51), the reader
will find that the immortality of Adonais consists of his being one
of 'the kings of thought/Who . . ./. . . of the past are all that
cannot pass away' (430–2).

Having thus asserted the only possible immortality to consist in
being a 'king of thought' such as Adonais is, the poet proceeds
convincingly to the rhetorical question, 'What Adonais is, why fear
we to become?' (459). Kings of thought, clearly, are those whose
minds have not permitted the events of life to determine the
progress and direction of their thought but have directed their own
thought in relation to those events. Because of the quality and the
productions of that thought, their influence prevails when in a
state of 'lofty thought' a young heart is the setting of the crucial
struggle between love and life. And such a king's influence will
align itself with the former of these two contestants. Love, being
the knowledge enormous of full and uncalculating involvement in
humanity, is the 'shadow of the tomb' in which the reader is
advised to take refuge. To the majority of people, who live the
dream called life, this loving knowledge has the appearance of
death because its participation in the great One is directly contrary
to the separate ego-identity that they call living. But since it consists
in the very opposite of ego-gratification and self-interest, it is in
actuality only the *shadow* of death and is the only refuge from, the
only avoidance of, death in the universe. A king of thought has
the power of will to choose and to direct others toward this life-in-
death condition of triumphant existence in and through participation in the great One.

There follows then the well-known stanza 52:

The One remains, the many change and pass;
Heaven's light forever shines, Earth's shadows fly;
Life, like a dome of many-coloured glass,
Stains the white radiance of Eternity,
Until Death tramples it to fragments. – Die,

If thou wouldst be with that which thou dost seek!
Follow where all is fled! – Rome's azure sky,
Flowers, ruins, statues, music, words, are weak
The glory they transfuse with fitting truth to
    speak.

This great One, which remains when all else changes and passes, is really three-in-one. In the preceding stanzas the poet has used the terms *thought, death* and *love* interchangeably, and in stanza 52 they are unified as the One. *Life*, as in stanza 44, is that which must be trampled down so that this trinity (lofty thought, death to materialistic values, and humanity-encompassing love) may be experienced as the 'white radiance of Eternity'. The imperative 'Die, / If thou wouldst be with that which thou dost seek!' can, then, not be read as an urging toward physical death.[19] The reader is directed to 'Follow where all is fled'. If all has not fled into physical death, where will we find ourselves when we have followed? We will find ourselves in our own consciousness or mental perceptions; that is, after all, where 'all is fled'. The sky, flowers, ruins, statues, music and words that Shelley lists as substantive entities are in themselves too weak to realize the glory to which they can give significance.

The realization of this glory comes only through the human mind's consciousness of these substantive entities, only through the 'spirit of events'. The argument of the poem, by its study of the death and immortality of Adonais, has driven these things or actualities to take their stand and to find their perpetuity ultimately in the human mind. In stanza 52 the reader is exhorted to follow by entering into the only true and lasting reality, the reality in his or her own mind, to find what through imaginative identification is genuine truth for the individual. The stanza is another indication that Shelley grasped fully the import of that 'knowledge enormous' by which Apollo in Keats's *Hyperion* comprehends a limitless range of substantive entities and thus becomes immortal.

The final three stanzas of *Adonais* transform the imperative 'follow where all is fled' into an irresistible invitation. The poet asks his heart, his centre of love, why it should linger in the false, disuniting existence called life when the uniting force of immortal thought (which he names successively Light, Beauty, Benediction and Love) beams upon him, removing the clouds of mortality that have kept him from seeing life clearly for what it is. The power of

Adonais's beaconing soul is the ability to remove obstructions to vision or understanding. His soul comes 'burning through' even the 'inmost veil' to invite the poet also to commit himself wholly to 'the abode where the Eternal are'.[20] As we have seen in stanza 44, that abode is not a distant allegorical heaven, but rather, the realm of highest thought where the ultimately consequential decisions are made.[21] At the conclusion of the poem, then, Shelley is being drawn with increased confidence to the goal toward which his entire life has tended: the goal of attaining the truth of his own loving, humanity-committed thought and of a simultaneous dissolution of all the claims upon him of conventionally valued motives of profit and power.

Thus Shelley supplies in *Adonais* a positive resolution of the human confrontation of life and death that in poems such as *Alastor* and 'Sonnet: Lift not the painted veil' arrives at problematic conclusions. Although the young *Alastor* Poet leaves the realm of conventional life to pursue a vision, we are given to see at the point of his death that his vision is only a reflection of the true, humanity-oriented love that would have filled his need. This young Poet is, indeed, identical with the individual in 'Sonnet: Lift not the painted veil' who dares to look behind the deceptions of life but does not or cannot supply any mental counter to the emptiness, the mutually negating pressures of hope and fear, that he finds there. The mythologized theme of the mind's sufficiency for love is developed in Shelley's poetry to the point at which the poet can clearly see its essential agreement with Keats's major theme and can articulate it with assurance in *Adonais*.

Shelley's conviction at the end of *Adonais* is that he must increasingly die out of what is generally called life and into his own mind-generated milieu of love. Not at all recording a tone of despair, the final stanzas are in full accord with stanza 39 and with the poem's other positive assertions about the mind and immortality such as the one by which stanza 44 illuminates the entire elegy: that actions based on imaginative love, instead of on materialistic calculation, do indeed constitute a life eternal.

4

The Emphasis on Social Enlightenment

An often-neglected sonnet may serve well to introduce our study of the emphasis that, relying on the strength of human thought and love, Shelley placed on social enlightenment. It is 'Sonnet: To the Republic of Benevento' – better known as 'Political Greatness', the title which Mary Shelley gave the sonnet when she first published it in 1824. The sonnet reads as follows:

> Nor happiness nor majesty nor fame
> Nor peace nor strength nor skill in arms or arts
> Shepherd those herds whom Tyranny makes tame;
> Verse echoes not one beating of their hearts,
> History is but the shadow of their shame –
> Art veils her glass, or from the pageant starts
> As to Oblivion their blind millions fleet,
> Staining that Heaven with obscene imagery
> Of their own likeness. – What are numbers knit
> By force or custom? Man who man would be,
> Must rule the empire of himself; in it
> Must be supreme, establishing his throne
> On vanquished will, – quelling the anarchy
> Of hopes and fears, – being himself alone. –

The opening image of the sonnet is that of 'herds' that are shepherded not by happiness, majesty, fame, peace, strength, or military or artistic skills, but by 'Tyranny'. These oblivion-bound masses of humanity, the sonnet goes on to say, cast only a shadow of shame in the records of history and stain the 'Heaven' of art's mirror with their obscene reflection, causing art to avoid dealing with them. There follows the rhetorical question of lines 9 and 10 that underscores the worthlessness and nothingness already ascribed to these millions. In response to this question, the poet ends the sonnet with a declaration and explanation of the value or meaning of the individual mind's conscious, willing use of its essential autonomy.

To rule the empire of oneself involves the seeming paradox of vanquishing the will. But Shelley supplies immediately an explanatory appositive; the 'anarchy of hopes and fears' describes the state of self-interested calculation that must be overcome or 'quelled'. The term *will*, then, stands here for wilfully seeking an advantage for the self, which involves a schizophrenic state of hoping for victory while simultaneously fearing, or being ashamed of, the defeat of true humanity inherent in such a victory. The focus in such a divided state cannot be constant, cannot be on what is genuinely true in one's vision of the world. It is truth to the individual's genuine perception that is expressed by the phrase 'being himself alone' – the sonnet's concluding explanation of how one is to rule and be supreme in the empire of oneself. To be oneself alone is to be what Shelley in 'Ode to Liberty' (243) designates as a 'King of Life' and what in *Adonais*, as we have seen, he terms a 'king of thought'. The concept of kingship is clearly articulated in the sonnet's use of 'to rule the empire . . .'. As in 'Ode to Liberty' and *Adonais*, life and will are here equated with each other, constituting that which should not dominate the individual but that needs to be under the control of the individual's freely determining mind.

Looking ahead to 'The Triumph of Life', we may not be far afield if we find 'Political Greatness' anticipating the predominant question – 'Then what is Life?' – of Shelley's last, fragmentary poem. The sonnet supplies an answer that Shelley might well have reiterated had he completed 'The Triumph of Life'. Throughout his works, the need for self-knowledge and intellectually-stirred self-direction, which is, after all, the essence of true responsibility – to be directed by humane motives as natural phenomena are directed by Necessity – is the basis of Shelley's politics of social enlightenment. As Timothy Webb asserts, 'Responsibility is, in fact, the keynote of much of Shelley's political poetry' (121). Symbolized by the yearly cycle of the Adonis myth in *Adonais*, Necessity remains for Shelley the operative force in nature. In human affairs (as distinct from natural phenomena) he considers that humane motivation such as the ultimate sense of responsibility urged by Demogorgon at the end of *Prometheus Unbound*, instead of self-centred calculation, is the only way to remain within the scope of the moral equivalent of Necessity. Here Dawson's commentary is to the point:

> History is only on the side of those who use good means to produce good ends. Used in this way 'Necessity' has none of the quietist overtones present in Godwin's reliance on it. Shelley holds up Necessity as a warning to those who are committed to political action. (98)

'Politics', as Webb conjectures, 'were probably the dominating concern in Shelley's intellectual life' (75). The first noteworthy poem of Shelley's comprehensive political emphasis is *Queen Mab*, which, so far as overt, discernible effects are concerned, appears historically to have had as great an effect on society as any other of his works. It touched and inspired the Chartists of the mid-nineteenth century in a kinetic way and to an effect whose importance no amount of aesthetic condemnation of this early work has been able to diminish.[1] The source of this effect must lie in the genuineness of feeling and the correlation of the poem's successful artistic devices with the human condition of its nineteenth-century readers. When these readers, relatively unconcerned with aesthetic refinement, came upon Shelley's artistic treatment of the world of their troubles and of what should be done about it, they responded enthusiastically to what their experience told them was true and genuine in the poem.

Consisting almost entirely of Queen Mab's admonishments to the awakened spirit of the sleeping Ianthe, this long poem is an early example of what, in the sonnet 'Political Greatness' Shelley declares to be the responsibility of the mind. Repeatedly, Queen Mab tells Ianthe to look at things directly and openly, to trust what her own eyes see and, banishing the hopes-and-fears anarchy, to set out to change the world for the better – which is after all, in Shelley's ultimate poetry, what is achieved by Prometheus.[2] That Shelley, already at this early stage of his career, was working successfully toward the theme of *Prometheus Unbound*, the theme of the necessary union of love and intellect, is shown at the very outset in the poem's dedicatory verses addressed to Harriet. Asking rhetorically whose loving eyes have made him love 'mankind the more', the poet answers that they are Harriet's and that she has been his 'purer mind'. Thus, very like the emphasis in 'Political Greatness', his stress is on the real importance of genuine love, which lies in its being of the mind and operating in the interaction between minds to extend itself to reach the world in which people live.

In her very first speech, rousing Ianthe's spirit for a journey among the spheres to be shown the realities of the universe, Queen Mab anticipates the sonnet's emphasis on the need to vanquish wilful self-interest and to trust one's own mind to direct the will. She declares Ianthe to be in the first rank of 'Those who have struggled, and with resolute will/Vanquished earth's pride and meanness' (1.125–6). Introducing herself to Ianthe as keeper of the wonders of the world, Queen Mab identifies 'the unfailing consciences' of human beings as her source of this knowledge from out of the past (1.170). Her role as true poet, or prophet, is made clear as she continues:

> The future, from the causes which arise
> In each event, I gather . . .
> > . . . that the spirit
> Clothed in its changeless purity, may know
> How soonest to accomplish the great end
> For which it hath its being, and may taste
> That peace, which in the end all life will share.
>
> > > (1.172–85)

Shelley thus shows her to be the poetic intellect that pays close and honest attention to the events of life so that the loving spirit of humanity may have reliable material with which to work and factual knowledge of the functioning of the world that is in need of renovation.

Emphasizing, in section 2, what is to be gained from the past, Queen Mab sets down her view of what should be the primary aim of historical study: 'Learn to make others happy' (64). To the elemental importance and responsibility of the human mind in the historic process of time she gives expression in the lines,

> How wonderful! that even . . .
> > . . . the weak touch
> That moves the finest nerve,
> And in one human brain
> Causes the faintest thought, becomes a link

In the great chain of nature.

(2.102–8)

The past, Queen Mab points out, has failed dismally, has shown how perverse and corrupted mankind can be. Having designated as 'fiends' the masses who have willingly subjected themselves to the rule of legendary and historical monarchs, she asks rhetorically,

> But what was he who taught them that the God
> Of nature and benevolence hath given
> A special sanction to the trade of blood?

(2.155–7)

And she finally lays on 'wealth, that curse of man,' the essential blame for this sanctioning of warfare. Wealth, she says, had driven away 'Virtue and wisdom, truth and liberty' (2.204–6).

The spirit of Ianthe thankfully declares at the outset of part 3 what she has gained from what Queen Mab has shown her of the past:

> I know
> The past, and thence I will essay to glean
> A warning for the future, so that man
> May profit by his errors, and derive
> Experience from his folly:
> For, when the power of imparting joy
> Is equal to the will, the human soul
> Requires no other Heaven.

(3.6–13)

To show how far the human society still is from having either the power or the will to impart joy, Queen Mab responds by renewing her emphasis on the cruel disregard of human need that is characteristic of despotic rulers. She depicts verbally a sumptuously clothed king secluded in his gorgeous, heavily guarded palace, giving no heed to the curses, groans and shrieks of the suffering poor outside. This disregard he achieves by a willful means of self-deception:

> When he hears
> The tale of horror, to some ready-made face
> Of hypocritical assent he turns,
> Smothering the glow of shame, that, spite of him,
> Flushes his bloated cheek.

(3.40–4)

Yet she sees that such a man of power is unable to find joy; instead, he seems to 'hug / The scorpion that consumes him' (3.87–8). Nor do the masses appear willing to rebel against their subjection to a ruler who evidences such perverted thought and conduct. This she does not, however, find to be strange, because

> He, like the vulgar, thinks, feels, acts and lives
> Just as his father did; the unconquered powers
> Of precedent and custom interpose
> Between a *king* and virtue.

(3.96–9)

What most irritates and rouses Queen Mab about this whole system, ingrained through the ages to favour the ironically unhappy rich and powerful, is that

> yon squalid form,
> Leaner than fleshless misery, that wastes
> A sunless life in the unwholesome mine,
> Drags out in labour a protracted death,
> To glut their grandeur; many faint with toil,
> That few may know the cares and woe of sloth.

(3.112–17)

It is not violent action but the mind of humanity, she declares, that must ultimately overcome this absurd system. Disregarding the playthings of its childhood, 'man's maturer nature' (3.131) will learn to disregard the dazzle and authority of kingly glare, and (Shelley here anticipating the conclusion of Act 3 of *Prometheus Unbound*) instead of being attacked and shattered, 'the gorgeous throne / Shall stand unnoticed in the regal hall, / Fast falling to decay' (3.134–6). Such disregard of power is the natural state of humanity, and only by returning to it can people avoid becoming more and more unnatural robots.

> Nature rejects the monarch, not the man;
> The subject, not the citizen: for kings
> And subjects, mutual foes, for ever play
> A losing game into each other's hands,
> Whose stakes are vice and misery. The man
> Of virtuous soul commands not, nor obeys.
> Power, like a desolating pestilence,
> Pollutes whate'er it touches; and obedience,
> Bane of all genius, virtue, freedom, truth,
> Makes slaves of men, and, of the human frame,
> A mechanized automaton.

> (3.170–80)

Queen Mab sums up this section of her discourse by tersely reasserting the unnatural perversity of mankind in its present state:

> The universe,
> In nature's silent eloquence, declares
> That all fulfil the works of love and joy –
> All but the outcast man. He fabricates
> The sword which stabs his peace; he cherisheth
> The snakes that gnaw his heart; he raiseth up
> The tyrant, whose delight is in his woe,
> Whose sport is in his agony.

> (3.196–203)

Sections 4 and 5 continue Queen Mab's analysis of the present condition of human society, her main theme being that not nature but the *choice* of evil that the human mind has made and continues to make is to blame for the perpetual agony in the world.

> Man's evil nature, that apology
> Which kings who rule, and cowards who crouch, set up
> For their unnumbered crimes, sheds not the blood
> Which desolates the discord-wasted land.

From kings, and priests, and statesmen, war arose . . .

(4.76–80)

In what is perhaps the poem's most graphic passage, Queen Mab makes her point by presenting a young child playing with a war toy which has been given the child by its elders along with an indoctrination as to its sanctioned use.

> Nature! – no!
> Kings, priests, and statesmen, blast the human flower
> Even in its tender bud . . .
> The child,
> Ere he can lisp his mother's sacred name,
> Swells with the unnatural pride of crime, he lifts
> His baby-sword even in a hero's mood.
> This infant-arm becomes the bloodiest scourge
> Of devastated earth; whilst specious names,
> Learnt in soft childhood's unsuspecting hour,
> Serve as the sophisms with which manhood dims
> Bright reason's ray, and sanctifies the sword
> Upraised to shed a brother's innocent blood.

(4.103–16)

The wealthy and pious advisors, whom she calls 'grave and hoary-headed hypocrites', receive Queen Mab's denunciation for their supplying tyrants with three words: 'God, Hell, and Heaven', by means of which the impressionable masses 'who dare belie / Their human nature' are made to 'cringe / Before the mockeries of earthly power' (4.203–20).

Closely connected to this religious emphasis on reward and punishment, says Queen Mab, is selfishness, 'Twin-sister of religion' (5.22). The term she uses to designate the activity in which selfishness is manifest is *commerce*, defined as 'the venal interchange / Of all that human art or nature yield; / Which wealth should purchase not, but want demand' (5.38–40). Had today's terminology been available to Shelley, he would no doubt have used the term *profit motive*. What happens, Queen Mab continues, is that in this material interchange human life is sold, the labour of the masses and the conscription of soldiers being used to heap up luxuries for those who attain power. The effect upon society is that 'all free and generous love/Of enterprize and daring' is extinguished by a 'grovelling hope of interest and gold' (5.86–91).

What keeps the poor man who feels 'the horror of the tyrant's deeds' from rising up to laugh to scorn the rhetoric of tyranny which keeps him subjected is 'the arm of power, / That knows and dreads his enmity' (5.124–6). Designating society as 'a public mart/Of undisguising selfishness, that sets/On each its price', she sees that 'Even love is sold' (5.186–9) and laments that 'Without a shudder, the slave-soldier lends/His arm to murderous deeds' (5.206–7). Though she reminds Ianthe's spirit of the nobler 'consciousness of good, which neither gold, / Nor sordid fame, nor hope of heavenly bliss/Can purchase' (5.223–5), and though she believes that 'hoary-headed selfishness has felt/Its death-blow, and is tottering to the grave' (5.249–50), Queen Mab's focus throughout parts 4 and 5 is on the degradations and distortions that, due to the mind's acquiescences and its choices, still characterize human society.

In section 6, voicing her opposition to the mind-forged God-concept that permits and abets this debasement of society, Queen Mab makes her strongest argument for Necessity as the operative power that the human mind must acknowledge. The 'eternal world', which in Shelley's view is the world of the mind, 'Contains at once the evil and the cure' (6.31–2). The evil lies in the mental concoction of a religion that bends all causes to embodiment in a self-sufficing, omnipotent God who is simply the 'prototype of human misrule' (6.105). The cure is to be found in the mind's learning to operate in accordance with Necessity, the force whom Queen Mab addresses as 'mother of the world' (6.198).

Gerald McNiece comes close to a full identification of Shelley's view of Necessity as it is reflected in *Queen Mab*. Shelley, as McNiece points out (*Revolutionary Idea*, 142–4), considers nature as the process in which 'in no case could any event have happened otherwise than it did happen'.[3] Human beings, however, through the perverting influence of kings and priests, have stepped out of their rightful alignment with nature. All that needs to be added to McNiece's analysis is the point that the original blame for this misalignment lies in perverted human thought, which (thought being free to choose among motives) is the one element in all nature that can wreak havoc in the world. Perverted thought has instituted and given power to kings and priests, thus placing human beings in a condition that is miserable because it will continue to be buffeted by Necessity until the human mind can get back in line and, doing away with kingship and priestcraft, can flow with the universal current of Necessity.

Shelley's contention that, when they cease to infringe natural law, human beings may experience endless springtime is premised essentially on the necessity of self-reform. Stating unequivocally in his Notes to the poem that 'motive is to voluntary action in the human mind what cause is to effect in the material universe' (*Poetical Works*, 809),[4] Shelley makes one point very clear: the urgently needed revolution is a change in the motives that govern the choices made by the human mind. Woodring's commentary, though made in reference to *The Revolt of Islam*, speaks to that point:

> Necessity means to him what the doctrine of consequences meant to George Eliot: since no act can be recovered and every action has numberless consequences, you must in consequence acquire as much knowledge, sympathy, and empathy as you can in order to meliorate consequences to every act you contemplate.
>
> (256)

Instead of continuing to serve the perverted motive of self-interest, mankind must learn how to identify with others and to adopt the motive of loving, symbiotic relationships.

Clearly distinguishing Necessity from 'human sense' and 'human thought' (6.618–19), Queen Mab depicts the raising of a shrine in honour of this power, an enduring shrine impervious to the erosion of time's tidal movements. This shrine she identifies as 'The sensitive extension of the world' (6.231), meaning the action of the mind that, without prejudice, proceeds from the observation of events in the realm of nature's necessity to relate imaginatively with all that is not self. Shelley goes out of his way to make sure that readers will not interpret this shrine as another dogmatic, stolid institution being set up by Queen Mab in place of the old one she has just denounced. He has her explain its mutable essence not as structured but, rather, as analogous to the process of oxidation caused by fire:

> That wondrous and eternal fane . . .
> Like hungry and unresting flame

Curls round the eternal columns of its strength.

(6.232–8)

The flame imagery is highly appropriate to a depiction of imaginative, loving mental activity, which perpetually needs its fuel yet, as Shelley was later to assert in 'Mont Blanc' regarding intellectual perception, must depend on certain supporting principles ('columns of its strength') in order to constitute a structure, however changeable and changing. Those columns are the essential metaphorical iconography of the truth that there is a natural, continuing pattern of causality – of one event having a bearing upon another – in the world.

This truth, and not a misty fabrication of an unknown anthropomorphic tyrant in an abstract realm, says Queen Mab, must become the active concern of the human mind. As is reiterated early in the next part of the poem, 'The exterminable spirit it contains / Is nature's only God' (7.23–4). The shrine raised to nature's essential spirit of necessity is not a place for the mind to indulge in self-abasement and prostrate worship but an arena of interaction and involvement with flame-like motion. Instead of succumbing to awed, irresponsible, subjected worship of an inscrutable and omnipotent God, the mind is capable of allying itself with the strength of the necessity behind things and events and of becoming a force to help direct their aims and outcomes. Thus the term *shrine* takes on a creatively vibrant new meaning, and the concept of worship deserts its assumed role of static adoration to reveal its true nature: vital action.

After Ahasuerus, the Wandering Jew, called up by Queen Mab, has throughout most of part 7 verified for Ianthe's spirit what Queen Mab has said regarding humanity's failure in the past and present to achieve anything near its potentiality (especially as this failure stems from the acceptance of religious tyranny), Queen Mab turns, in part 8, to the subject of the future. Reviewing in condensed form the limitations of mankind that she has earlier elaborated upon, she sums up the human condition with the metaphorical assertion,

All was inflicted here that earth's revenge
Could wreck on the infringers of her law.

(8.163–4)

The world is 'ever-varying', and mankind can in the future, through the mind's action, cease to inhibit natural progress and can, instead, be a part and indeed the loftiest aspect of it.

> But chief, ambiguous man, he that can know
> More misery, and dream more joy than all;
> Whose keen sensations thrill within his breast
> To mingle with a loftier instinct there . . .
> Who stands amid the ever-varying world,
> The burthen or the glory of the earth;
> He chief perceives the change, his being notes
> The gradual renovation, and defines
> Each movement of its progress on his mind.

(8.134–44)

As humankind will learn to cooperate with nature, to accept the essential equality of all entities in the universe, to achieve peace and health as a cooperative force in nature, it will become evident, as Queen Mab foresees, that

> . . . every shape and mode of matter lends
> Its force to the omnipotence of mind,
> Which from its dark mine drags the gem of truth
> To decorate its paradise of peace.

(8.235–8)

In the poem's final section, Queen Mab enlarges upon the results of the mind's assumption of its rightful omnipotence – its triumph over systems of power and of religious mystery. She speaks of

> Courage of soul, that dreaded not a name,
> And elevated will, that journeyed on
> Through life's phantasmal scene in fearlessness . . .
> . . . that sweet bondage which is freedom's self,
> And rivets with sensation's softest tie
> The kindred sympathies of human souls.

(9.72–9)

The reader needs to be aware that 'sensation's softest tie', whatever it may sound like to the modern ear, is not to be equated with sentimentalism of any kind but means, rather, as in the above-noted line 'The sensitive extension of the world' (5.231), the mind's simply and gently taking what the senses perceive in necessity-infused nature and generating from this the impulses to action. Queen Mab is confident that, when the mind takes on this its proper role, necessary and beneficial improvements such as the disappearance of the need for 'tyrannic law' and for the checks of 'dull and selfish chastity', as well as the emergence of 'Woman and man, in confidence and love,/Equal and free and pure together' (9.79–90), will result.

Queen Mab's long exhortation does not end in flights of unrealistic fantasy; instead, she emphasizes 'The gradual paths of an aspiring change' (9.148) and encourages the spirit of Ianthe to bear on bravely, to know that her will

> Is destined an eternal war to wage
> With tyranny and falsehood, and uproot
> The germs of misery from the human heart.
>
> (9.189–92)

And finally, in the imagery of the brow and the focus upon the seemingly imprisoned will, the emphasis is on the human mind's responsibility and its options:

> Thine is the brow whose mildness would defy
> Its [tyranny's] fiercest rage, and brave its
>   sternest will,
> When fenced by power and master of the world . . . .
> Earth's pride and meanness could not vanquish thee.
>
> (9.197–203)

These lines, very nearly the last that Queen Mab speaks in the poem, have identically the emphasis of the sonnet 'Political Greatness', the discussion of which opens the present chapter. The will, though caught and surrounded by the power of pride and meanness, can be liberated. The will is subject to the mind, which can reverse even its own conditioned tendencies and can always discern the way of liberty – to which *Queen Mab* is totally dedicated. As is shown in Webb's effective tracing (85–7) of Shelley's correspondence regarding *Queen Mab*, he never, over the years, backed away from its central theme of the political necessity of mind-tested liberty.

In *The Revolt of Islam* Shelley takes up the subject of how the mind-directed will is actually to be applied to the project of overcoming tyranny. As already made clear in *Queen Mab*, the way of the sword cannot ultimately achieve this triumph. The mind must find a new revolutionary method, and the will must be energetic and strong enough to put it into practice. Laon and Cythna, the co-protagonists of *The Revolt of Islam*, have the imaginative creativity to devise the necessary mental revolution as well as the stamina or staying power to keep on applying and practicing it. In the face of repeated rebuffs that follow temporary successes, they persevere until finally, at the scene of their shared martyr death, there is at least the prophetic 'murmur . . . / Of deep and mighty change' (4718–19). The method that they discover and practice is that of nonviolent resistance and activism – a concept to which Shelley had first given strong, outspoken expression in his prose *Address to the Irish People* in 1812 and which was the logical concomitant of his growing emphasis both on the autonomy of the human mind and on the mind's need to become one with love, the union that is grandly celebrated later in *Prometheus Unbound*.

Unhesitatingly, Shelley declares in his Preface to *The Revolt of Islam* that he has sought to enlist the various artistic devices of poetry 'in the cause of a liberal and comprehensive morality' and that his poem is 'a succession of pictures illustrating the growth and progress of individual mind aspiring after excellence, and devoted to the love of mankind', which results in 'the awakening of an immense nation from their slavery and degradation to a true sense of moral dignity and freedom'.[5] That such an awakening was not achieved historically by the French Revolution, he asserts, has been a large part of the instigation for the poem.[6] His point is that there is a better way than was available to the French revolutionaries, who had after all been 'dupes and slaves for centuries' and therefore were 'incapable of conducting themselves with the wisdom and tranquility of freemen so soon as some of their fetters were partially loosened' (33). Shelley's perspective is very close to, and perhaps derived in large part from, the thinking of the youthful Coleridge, who declared, 'That general illumination should precede revolution, is a truth as obvious, as that the vessel should be cleansed before we fill it with a pure liquor.'[7]

The alternatives that Shelley's poem is meant to assert are clearly evident in the rhetorical questions that, as if underscoring Coleridge's view, he raises about the French Revolution:

> Could they listen to the plea of reason who had groaned under the calamities of a social state according to the provisions of which one man riots in luxury whilst another famishes for want of bread? Can he who the day before was a trampled slave suddenly become liberal-minded, forbearing, and independent?
> (33)

Responsiveness to reason, liberal-mindedness, forbearance and independence come about, Shelley explicitly states, 'by resolute perseverance and indefatigable hope, and long-suffering and long-believing courage, and the systematic efforts of generations of men of intellect and virtue' (33). Thus, what Queen Mab has commanded the spirit of Ianthe to perform Shelley means in *The Revolt of Islam* to set before us in an imaginative context of active commitment in the world of historic reality. And the revolutionary nature of what Laon and Cythna attempt Shelley reiterates with unmistakable clarity as he brings the Preface to conclusion:

> In recommending also a great and important change in the spirit which animates the social institutions of mankind, I have avoided all flattery to those violent and malignant passions of our nature which are ever on the watch to mingle with and to alloy the most beneficial innovations. There is no quarter given to Revenge, or Envy, or Prejudice. Love is celebrated everywhere as the sole law which should govern the moral world.   (37)

By far Shelley's longest poetic work, *The Revolt of Islam* is essentially Laon's account of how he and his stepsister-lover Cythna expound and endeavour, with inconsistent degrees of success and with uneven results, to replace the violent and malignant passions with the law of love as the determinant of human action.[8] What first stirs Laon to be the exponent of this revolution is the absolute repugnance that, Hamlet-like, he feels toward the generally accepted world-as-it-is:

> This vital world, this home of happy spirits,
>   Was as a dungeon to my blasted kind;
> All that despair from murdered hope inherits
>   They sought, and in their helpless misery blind,
>   A deeper prison and heavier chains did find,
> And stronger tyrants.
>
>   (712–17)

Very early Laon sees that the reason for this deplorable condition is that thinking people have resigned their prerogative of self-responsible thought and have, as Shelley later presents Prometheus as having done, relegated this highest of human glories and obligations to an oppressive god-figure:

> For they all pined in bondage; body and soul,
>   Tyrant and slave, victim and torturer, bent
> Before one Power, to which supreme control
>   Over their will by their own weakness lent,
>   Made all its many names omnipotent.
>
>   (730–4)

Declaring that 'It shall be thus no more' and that he 'will arise and waken / The multitude' (775–85), Laon becomes a writer of extraordinary power to sway an audience. His writings, 'thoughts invested with the light / Of language,' are such a luminous testimony that 'all bosoms made reply / On which its lustre streamed . . .' (807–9).

After, however, the apparent inconsistency and unfaithfulness of a particular friend who has been especially involved with him in these ideas, Laon finds that only one person is left to him as full and equal devotee of the cause. This person is Cythna, whom he introduces thus:

> An orphan with my parents lived, whose eyes
>   Were lodestars of delight, which drew me home
> When I might wander forth.
>
>   (847–9)

Addressing her directly, he introduces the essential element of her being, basic to the theme of the poem:

> Even then, methought, with the world's tyrant rage
> A patient warfare thy young heart did wage.

> (859–60)

That the two become equal in strength to oppose and to innovate is not mere coincidence in the poem. Shelley's purpose simultaneously to further the cause of personal renovation as well as the cause of women's liberation is made very clear in Laon's words,

> Never will peace and human nature meet
> Till free and equal man and woman greet
> Domestic peace; and ere this power can make
> In human hearts its calm and holy seat,
> This slavery [woman's servitude] must be broken.

> (994–8)

Cythna not only echoes Laon's words but, as if Mary Wollstonecraft herself were speaking, makes the point more emphatically:

> Can man be free if woman be a slave? . . .
> Can they whose mates are beasts, condemned to bear
> Scorn, heavier far than toil or anguish, dare
> To trample their oppressors?

> (1045–50)[9]

But, of course, the desired trampling of oppressors is not to take the form of the old, discredited physically violent subduing.

Shelley seeks to present a breakthrough that in all the world's greatest civilizations has not been achieved – the peaceful attainment of sexual as well as socio-economic equality. Even the Greek society that he so greatly admired had treated women as inferior to men. In his essay 'On the Manners of the Ancient Greeks' he declares, though, that his own society has less excuse than did the Greeks for not abolishing the 'invidious distinction of humankind as a class of beings of intellectual nature into two sexes' – a distinction that he terms 'a remnant of savage barbarism' (*Shelley's Prose*, 223). As Webb has shown (194), this sexual discrimination, together with a dependence on the existence of an underprivileged slave class, was a blot on the idealism and on the glorious monuments of the Golden Age of Greece, which was finally undermined by its reliance upon the very system of revenge and retribution against which Aeschylus so often had warned the people of his country.

Through Laon and Cythna, Shelley surely hopes to be an even more successful voice to modern civilization than was Aeschylus to the ancient one. He knows that for this to occur he must genuinely win the mind of humanity. Anticipating her separation from Laon, perhaps even their respective deaths in the pursuit of their cause, Cythna asserts that the battle is to take place in and for the minds of people:

> We meet again
> Within the minds of men, whose lips shall bless
> Our memory, and whose hopes its light retain
> When these dissevered bones are trodden in the
> plain.

(1095–8)

The narrative progression of the poem need not be recounted here. Suffice it to say that, having survived their separate ordeals of daring and persecution, each having made grand strokes for the nonviolent revolution (Laon himself in desperation not having remained literally and absolutely true to the principle of non-violence[10]), the two are reunited and retire to a secluded mountain ruin, away from a world fallen into chaos because of humanity's irrational continuance in its violent ways. In the course of his adventures, Laon has been revived and heartened by an old Godwinian hermit, a disciple of his, whose words show how well he has read Laon's writings:

> If blood be shed, 'tis but a change and choice
> Of bonds, – from slavery to cowardice
> A wretched fall!

(1657–9)

And Laon, having interposed himself between two battling foes, thus receiving a spear wound in his arm, has declaimed to the deeply impressed armies surrounding him,

> Oh wherefore should ill ever flow from ill,
>   And pain still keener pain forever breed?
> We all are brethern – even the slaves who kill
>   For hire, are men; and to avenge misdeed
>   On the misdoer, doth but Misery feed
> With her own broken heart!

> (1810–15)

Later he has dissuaded a crowd from wreaking vengeance on even the fallen tyrant himself by crying out to them that 'the chastened will/Of virtue sees that justice is the light/Of love, and not revenge, and terror and despite' (2023–5).

After Laon and Cythna have been reunited and have physically as well as spiritually consummated their love, Cythna relates in detail to Laon the story of her experience since their separation. The wondrous success that she has had in turning people toward the law of love has resulted essentially from the ideas that she has disseminated in grand oratory among the people. Covering the scope and sweep of the goals that she and Laon share, her long message, as she recalls it in detail for Laon, may be summed up in the following lines:

> O Love, who to the hearts of wandering men
> Art as the calm to Ocean's weary waves!
>   Justice, or Truth, or Joy! those only can
>   From slavery and religion's labyrinth caves
>   Guide us, as one clear star the seaman saves.
>   . . .
>   Ye might arise, and will
>   That gold should lose its power, and thrones their glory;
> That love, which none may bind, be free to fill
>   The world, like light; and evil faith, grown hoary
>   With crime, be quenched and die.
>   . . .
>   It is the dark idolatry of self,
>   Which, when our thoughts and actions once are gone,
>   Demands that man should weep, and bleed, and groan;

O vacant expiation! Be at rest. –
  The past is Death's, the future is thine own;
  And love and joy can make the foulest breast
A paradise of flowers, where peace might build her nest.

                           (3289–396)

The importance given, in the last of these segments, to thoughts linked with actions should again not be overlooked. Throughout the poem the pre-eminent place is given to the process of thought that leads to action for the betterment of society. By the same token, the enemies of virtue are shown to be, first and foremost, fearful of, and enraged against, free and open thought. Of the prideful Iberian Priest, zealous instigator of Laon and Cythna's execution, we are told,

He loathed all faith beside his own, and pined
To wreak his fear of Heaven in vengeance on Mankind.

But more he loathed and hated the clear light
  Of wisdom and free thought, and more did fear,
Lest, kindled once, its beams might pierce the night,
  Even where his Idol stood.

                           (4079–84)

The freedom that comes when people trust and follow free thought, as Laon praises the Americans for having done (4415–40), is essentially a freedom from enslavement to cold materialism, symbolized by luxury and gold.[11] And it is an opening of the liberty genuinely to experience love and joy (4376–86).

Because of the mental nature of the basic revolution that Laon and Cythna strive for, even their execution is not their defeat. There is, after all, as they die, 'a murmur from the crowd' that tells of thought's continuing action – of a 'deep and mighty change which suddenly befell' (4718–19). As with the metaphorical symbol of Padua's fires in 'Lines Written among the Euganean Hills', there is bound to be another outcropping so long as people are susceptible to the urgings of their own free thought. And, who knows, the next time it may come closer than does the thought-and-action of

Laon and Cythna to a full achievement of the goal that Queen Mab sets before the spirit of Ianthe.

No event in history could have been tailored more exactly than was the Manchester Massacre to reinforce the thought and to rouse in Shelley again the spirit that had produced *Queen Mab* and *The Revolt of Islam*. It was at Manchester on 16 August 1819 that a protest meeting of English workers, who had assembled peaceably in an area known as St. Peter's Field, was broken up by a cavalry charge in which six or more persons were killed and at least eighty (perhaps several hundred) wounded. In far-off Italy, moved by what he called 'the torrent of my indignation . . . boiling in my veins' (*Letters*, 2.117), Shelley composed the vibrant 'Mask of Anarchy', a poem simple in form but charged with all the philosophic energy that went into the composition of the earlier, much larger, and more complicated works.

The poem's first twenty stanzas give full vent to the outraged fury that news of the massacre stirred in Shelley. Comparing the personified vices Murder, Fraud and Hypocrisy, respectively, to Lord Castlereagh (the Foreign Secretary), Baron Eldon (the Lord Chancellor) and Viscount Sidmouth (the Home Secretary), the poet presents them as parading through England in disdain and derision of the ironically abject, fawning multitude. These three are accompanied in 'this ghastly masquerade' by a fourth horseman, Anarchy 'Like Death in the Apocalypse' (33), and by 'many more Destructions', who are 'all disguised, even to the eyes, / Like Bishops, lawyers, peers, or spies' (26–9). Anarchy, riding on a 'white horse, splashed with blood', and bearing on his brow the inscription, 'I am God, and King, and Law!' (30–7), represents Shelley's concept of distorted or unnatural government. It is anarchy because the many, who are the only rightful agents of power and government, are abjectly servile, while the privileged few, whose wealth and arrogance in every way disqualify them for the position of control, have usurped total authority. Castlereagh, Eldon, and Sidmouth, as well as the other figures of governmental and ecclesiastical order or system, are all serving in the vanguard of this anarchistically distorted system. In the opening section of the poem Shelley bitterly and sardonically castigates the whole structure of this anarchic system in which the few hold sway over the many, in which the rich and powerful dominate and oppress the poor, dispossessed masses. Such an arrangement, the direct antithesis to a system based on power rightfully in the hands of the people, is for him a detested mask – in the double sense of a paraded display of tyrannic power and of a false face that hides the essential anarchy.

As the abject masses echo back to Anarchy the adoring tribute, 'Thou art King, and God, and Lord' (71), Hope, a 'maniac maid', the last remaining daughter of Time, appears upon the scene as if she were Despair and lies down before the horses' feet.[12] She thus brings about the seemingly miraculous destruction of the whole masquerade (86–134).

The remainder of the poem consists of a lengthy pronouncement by the misty 'Shape'[13] that arises immediately after the defeat of Anarchy to speak in a voice that seems to arise from the earth 'As if her heart had cried aloud' (146). Addressing the 'Men of England, heirs of Glory' (147), the voice intones, at both the beginning and the end of the pronouncement, the exhortation,

> Rise like Lions after slumber
> In unvanquishable number –
> Shake your chains to Earth like dew
> Which in sleep had fallen on you –
> Ye are many – they are few.

The slumber imagery in this repeated stanza is of particular importance. While the mind has been inactive, while thought has not been stirring, the chains of subjection to an oppressive system administered by means of legalized violence have fallen upon the people. The poem's opening dramatic masque, ending not with mere optimism but with an active hope – a functioning of the wakeful mind opposing the distortions of materialism's oppressive juggernaut – serves well to introduce the voice's pronouncement of how power is to be rightfully reassumed by the people.

Defining for the people the slavery into which they have fallen, the voice emphasizes the essentially mental nature of the effect that their enslavement has had upon them. They have, the voice declares, been, with or without their 'own will', bent to their oppressor's 'defence and nourishment' (166–7), which is a prime indicator of what slavery is.

> 'Tis to be a slave in soul
> And to hold no strong controul

> Over your own wills, but be
> All that others make of ye.

(184–7)

Going on, by contrast, to define Freedom, the voice calls it by the names of Justice, Wisdom, Peace and Love – a Spirit, a Patience, a Gentleness that is lighted by the lamps of 'Science, Poetry, and Thought', whose loveliness needs to be expressed in 'deeds, not words' (209–61).

The deeds that express and further the cause of Freedom are not those of the violent, enslaving system that this cause opposes. When people are enslaved, the voice has said,

> Then it is to feel revenge
> Fiercely thirsting to exchange
> Blood for blood – and wrong for wrong –
> Do not thus when ye are strong.

(193–6)

Instead, if wisdom and love, as well as justice and peace, are to be united in one embodiment known as Freedom, a method diametrically opposite to the long-conditioned, vengeful response will have to be found. The voice advises,

> Let a great assembly be
> Of the fearless and the free . . .

> Let a vast assembly be,
> And with great solemnity
> Declare with measured words that ye
> Are, as God has made ye, free . . .

> And if then the tyrants dare
> Let them ride among you there,
> Slash, and stab, and maim, and hew, –
> What they like, that let them do.

With folded arms and steady eyes,
And little fear, and less surprise
Look upon them as they slay
Till their rage has died away.

(262–347)

This suggested assembly, clearly an echo of the mass meeting so viciously attacked in St. Peter's Field, is to have the added dimension of an intended strategy of resistance guided by the resolute yet essentially loving mind of the people, both as individuals and as a group. Indefatigably adhered to, this method, the voice assures Englishmen, will cause the tyrants to return in shame and to be spitefully rejected by the people. True soldiers will turn from the tyrants to join with the free non-violent populace, and the words of the repeated stanza that enjoins the people to 'Rise like lions after slumber' and to cast off their chains will be 'Ringing through each heart and brain' (366).[14] Especially noteworthy in the stanza is the emphasis on the 'heart' and the 'brain'. It is made clear that love and mind will have to coalesce so that a method other than the old, repetitive cycle of violence can be used by the many, who deserve to be free and who will be so if they can cast off the mental chains imposed on them by the few who have anarchistically suppressed freedom.

In 'The Mask of Anarchy' Shelley clearly and boldly anticipates Henry David Thoreau's *Civil Disobedience* and in so doing becomes the true pioneer, in imaginative literature written in the English language, of the concept of nonviolent resistance. That Thoreau read Shelley, that Gandhi quoted from 'The Mask of Anarchy' in the course of his nonviolent campaign in India,[15] and that Martin Luther King, Jr., acknowledged the influence of both Thoreau and Gandhi upon his non-violent campaign for civil rights in the United States are all testimonies to the achievement of at least a degree of that social effect that Shelley longed for his work to have.[16] In 'The Mask of Anarchy' the potentiality of this effect was destined to lie dormant until many years after Shelley's death, but it did achieve a degree of realization.

The freedom that both inspires and can result from the non-violent resistance of 'The Mask of Anarchy' is, in 'Ode to Liberty', traced through history and enthusiastically lauded as the light of life. For his metaphor the poet must use the source of light itself.

> One sun illumines heaven; one Spirit vast
> With life and love makes chaos ever new,
> As Athens doth the world with thy delight renew.

(88–90)

The great darknesses of history, the poet tells Liberty, have occurred because 'thou wert not' (23–38), and the great advances in enlightenment, from the rise of Greece onward have taken place because 'thou wert' (72).[17]

Adopting Athens ('. . . that hill/Which was thine earliest throne and latest oracle') as his symbol for the glory of Greek liberty, the poet presents it as a calm presence continuing to be reflected in the river of time:

> Within the surface of Time's river
> Its wrinkled image lies, as then it lay
> Immovably unquiet, and for ever
> It trembles, but it cannot pass away!

(76–9)

With effective reference to the recollected image of the calmness surrounding Peele Castle in Wordsworth's 'Elegiac Stanzas' as a partial parallel, Webb emphasizes, in contrast to Wordsworth's concern with the embodiment of a moral attitude, Shelley's desire to transmit through time and space a civilizing idea (223–4). Having seen the beam of liberty's light diminish and swell throughout history, he finds it ready again to reillumine the world's scene, if but its source can be made to function.

And again, as in other poems we have considered, the human mind is seen as the source of all potentiality:

> O, that the wise from their bright minds would kindle
> Such lamps within the dome of the dim world . . .
> O, that the words which make the thoughts obscure
> From which they spring . . .

Were stript of their thin masks and various hue . . .
Till in the nakedness of false and true
They stand before their Lord, each to receive its due!

(226–40)

But man, the individual person as well as the social group collectively, the poet declares, will find it a 'vain endeavor' to try to be the 'King of Life' he is meant to be,

If on his own high will, a willing slave,
He has enthroned the oppression and the oppressor.

(243–45)

So to have enthroned oppression and oppressor is to have succumbed to the 'dream of life', with its 'phantoms', 'mad trance' and 'invulnerable nothings', that is portrayed in stanza 39 of *Adonais*. The suggestion is unmistakable, in 'Ode to Liberty' as also in *Adonais*, 'Political Greatness' and 'The Triumph of Life', that only by an ethical, mental kingship over the issues and events of life can the individual, or the people collectively, maintain a level of existence worthy of humanity.

It is true, as Dawson points out (209–10), that this ode does not go beyond abstractions in its tribute to liberty. Nevertheless, though the lack of specific imagery certainly is its weakness, the ode attains a paean-like quality in its adoration of that value in human experience that Shelley so graphically illustrates in poems as diverse as 'Ode to the West Wind' and 'The Mask of Anarchy'. It envisions the glorious possibilities if but the mind would take seriously, rely upon and put into action its power of thought:

What if earth can clothe and feed
Amplest millions at their need,
And power in thought be as the tree within the seed?
Or what if Art, an ardent intercessor,
Diving on fiery wings to Nature's throne,
Checks the great mother stooping to caress her,
And cries: Give me, thy child, dominion
Over all height and depth? if Life can breed
New wants, and wealth from those who toil and groan

Rend of thy gifts and hers a thousandfold for one!

(246–55)

Here as in *Adonais* and 'The Triumph of Life', the term 'Life' is to be understood as the false, ego-centred mind-set that distorts true reality – a mind-set that has continued to our own time to permit starvation in one segment of society while in another there is a gross indulgence in superfluity of wealth. Shelley considers art to be rightfully the perceptive 'intercessor' whose role and duty it is to raise the questions that, assuming that clear thought leads to humane action, will no longer permit the false 'Life' to league with 'wealth' to set up superfluous wants and then to wrench from the toiling poor the means of obtaining them. If they would but demand from nature, the great mother, their proper dominion in the universe, the thought-engendered powers of liberty and art, united, might produce an as-yet-unheard-of harvest of gifts in the realm of human betterment.

The poet ends his address to Liberty by pleading with her to 'lead out of the inmost cave / Of man's deep spirit . . . / Wisdom'. If wisdom thus emerges, the 'Rulers of eternal thought' will take over their rightful position and will institute a society based on

> Blind Love, and equal Justice, and the Fame
> Of what has been, the Hope of what will be.

(256–65)

Not unmindful of the past and confident that better things can be in the future, this new society will be constituted on both Love and Justice – the true elements of Liberty.

In *Hellas*, one of his last poetic works, Shelley, more explicitly and emphatically than elsewhere, pronounces the 'rulers of eternal thought' to be the only rightful and ultimately successful powers in human society. In other words, he declares that people can, and therefore are obligated to, follow in action and structure the best that their minds in free pursuit of truth can imaginatively create.

Though he writes *Hellas* at the height of enthusiasm for the cause of Greece in its war for freedom from Turkish domination, Shelley makes of his poem a plea for and an excited expectation of a time when mental resistance and assault will replace violence in the battles for ever wider human freedoms. His support for the Greek cause may seem at times to spill over into support for the violent means that the Greeks employ, but the overriding emphasis and the climactic concluding affirmation of the poem indicate that, though he strongly supports the cause of Greek freedom, Shelley does not intend to advocate violence. With regard to both the classical basis of the poem and Shelley's intention with respect to the means of revolution, Webb presents a clarifying perspective:

> Aeschylus, of course, provides the basic pattern in his play the *Persae* which presents the effects of defeat in the battle of Salamis (480 B.C.) on the Persian court and emperor. . . . For Shelley's purposes this inherited framework provided an ideal perspective since it allowed him to adumbrate the possibilities of another Greek victory over the oriental enemy (in this case the Turks) without compromising his fundamental pacifism. *Hellas*, like the *Persae*, focuses on the psychology of defeat and is suffused with a sense of declared intention to celebrate the imminent recovery of Greek liberty. (199)

Unmistakably, the Prologue[18] establishes the ultimate, elemental reality of thought as the poem's theme. The Herald of Eternity declares that 'The dews of thought in the world's golden dawn / Earliest and most benign', have been the source of 'Temples and cities and immortal forms' and that from this source have sprung also further 'thoughts, and deeds worthy of thoughts so fair' (33–7). Then, in the face of Satan's counter-assertion that war, life's material trappings and tyranny will always triumph, the Christ of the Prologue asserts that 'the Power that wields and kindles' the worlds Satan speaks of is spiritual – of the mind, not material:

> True greatness asks not space, true excellence
> Lives in the Spirit of all things that live.

> (165–7)

And this assertion prepares the reader to trace the process of mental revolution that is the essence of *Hellas* itself. Although Richard Cronin (p. 135) perceptively suggests that, in the struggle between the Turks and the Greeks, both sides are destined to lose, he does not explain or develop the concept. Michael Scrivener (pp. 286–97), more fully discussing this poetic drama, perceives Shelley's underlying concern to be with the need for an ultimate system of nonviolence that will supercede and will provide a viable and renovating alternative to these hopeless, basically inconclusive military struggles.[19] Especially pertinent is Scrivener's assertion (296) that the 'brighter Hellas' of the drama's final chorus 'is not mystical, but altogether social . . . a genuine perception of the living imagination, thus necessarily different and better than the old Hellas'.

The progression of *Hellas* consists essentially of what Mahmud, emperor of the Turks, thinks and says in response to what he senses as a vast shift in human history. Symbolized for him in reports brought to him, first of the success of his forces against the Greeks and then of the direct reversal of the situation, this great shift becomes an unrelenting disturbance to Mahmud's complacency. At the outset he is distressed by a dream-vision of the disintegration of the power structure to which he has long been accustomed. What he sees is

> Ruin above, and anarchy below;
> Terror without, and treachery within;
> The chalice of destruction full, and all
> Thirsting to drink; and who among us dares
> To dash it from his lips? And where is Hope?

> (268–72)

Hassan, his magician-aide, assures him that 'The lamp of our dominion still rides high' (273) and gives him a lengthy report of the Turkish preparedness to crush the Greeks. Nevertheless, Mahmud cannot be brought out from under his cloud, his sense that the process of revolution is at work to undermine the entire framework within which his despotic regime has had meaning. The situation, in his view, is universal and desperate:

> Far other bark than ours were needed now
> To stem the torrent of descending time;
> The Spirit that lifts the slave before his lord
> Stalks through the capitals of armed kings

And spreads his ensign in the wilderness,
Exults in chains, and, when the rebel falls
Cries like the blood of Abel from the dust;
And the inheritors of the earth, like beasts
When earthquake is unleashed, with idiot fear
Cower in their kingly dens – as I do now.

(349–58)

Almost as if his vision might be prophetically piercing through to the ultimate upcoming irony implicit in continued power confrontations – the reliance on nuclear stockpiling for the purpose of deterring war – Mahmud adds the rehetorical questions,

What were Defeat when Victory must appal?
Or Danger when Security looks pale?

(359–60)

Hassan, despite his exultation over Turkish victories, has to admit that in what he has seen of the assurance and defiance of conquered Greeks, who made confident prophetic assertions and then died, there is much to support Mahmud's apprehensive forebodings. His account of his own experience in a naval battle in which the Greeks routed the Turks serves to underscore the feeling that the forces of thought and freedom may in all actuality be commencing their ascendancy. As if unmistakably to verify that this is precisely what is happening, messenger after messenger arrives, reporting Greek victory after Greek victory.

At this juncture comes the announcement of the arrival of Ahasuerus, the Wandering Jew, whom Mahmud has earlier bidden Hassan to summon for the purpose of dealing, from the perspective of his age-old experience, with the ominous present. But before Ahasuerus makes his commentary, there comes an interlude provided by the Chorus of Greek captive women. It is a lyric that celebrates the revolution of thought symbolized historically by Greece:

But Greece and her foundations are
Built below the tide of war,
Based on the crystalline sea

Of thought and its eternity.

(696–9)[20]

As the lyric continues, the image of a sudden, fierce battle is evoked.

I hear! I hear!
The crash as of an empire falling,
The shrieks as of a people calling
'Mercy? Mercy!' how they thrill!
Then a shout of 'Kill! Kill! Kill!'

(723–7)

Immediately a small still voice explains,

Revenge and wrong bring forth their kind,
The foul cubs like their parents are,
Their den is in the guilty mind
And Conscience feeds them with despair.

(729–32)

Since there is, then, obviously no hope in the old cycle of revenge and killing, essentially a construct of the mind, the chorus concludes that there must be a revolutionary return to an association, in the mind, of wisdom with pity or love, an association clearly symbolized in ancient Athens:

In sacred Athens, near the fane
Of Wisdom, Pity's altar stood.
Serve not the unknown God in vain,
But pay that broken shrine again,
Love for hate and tears for blood!

(733–7)

Thus the chorus gives voice to the very movement that, throughout the drama, Mahmud apprehensively senses in the atmosphere all about him.

What Ahasuerus tells him still further hammers home in Mahmud's mind the conviction that his old materialistic system of
power is doomed. From his storehouse of knowledge, filled
through the ages of his endless existence, Ahasuerus draws forth
a catalogue of images representing all that human beings generally
accept as the world of reality and declares that all of it

> Is but a vision – all that it inherits
> Are motes of a sick eye, bubbles and dreams;
> Thought is its cradle and its grave, nor less
> The future and the past are idle shadows
> Of thought's eternal flight – they have no being.
> Nought is but that which feels itself to be.
>   . . . Thought
> Alone, and its quick elements, Will, Passion,
> Reason, Imagination, cannot die;
> They are, what that which they regard, appears,
> The stuff whence mutability can weave
> All that it hath dominion o'er, worlds, worms,
> Empires and superstitions.

> (780–801)

If thought is all-important, then Mahmud's empire is really nothing.
And if the revolution now stirring is aimed at giving thought its
rightful, ruling place, then it must be a right and proper revolution,
one that shows Mahmud that his whole empire is but a dream.

Leaving this idea to develop in Mahmud's mind, Ahasuerus
departs, but not before he has introduced the Phantom of Mahomet
the Second – the phantom, that is, of the regime from the time of
its earliest strength. The Phantom assures Mahmud that his power
structure certainly is dying and adds, 'Woe! Woe! / To the weak
people tangled in the grasp / Of its last spasms' (891–3). This brings
on the point of Mahmud's total capitulation, his acceptance of the
revolution of thought as actual. First he cries out,

> Spirit, woe to all!
> Woe to the wronged and the avenger! woe
> To the destroyer; woe to the destroyed!
> Woe to the dupe; and woe to the deceiver!
> Woe to the oppressed; and woe to the oppressor!

> Woe both to those that suffer and inflict,
> Those who are born and those who die!

(893–9)

Addressing the phantom, in the next line, as 'Imperial shadow of the thing I am', Mahmud, as Terrence Hoagwood has shown, becomes, as is Prometheus in *Prometheus Unbound*, a dramatic instance of 'one mind's discovery that its superstitions are its own work and that its ghosts and gods are projections of itself' (170).

When suddenly there is another reversal in the tide of the present war and his forces outside shout 'Victory! Victory!' Mahmud demonstrates his new-found total disbelief in any victory through material strife. Just before his exit from the scene, he cries out,

> I must rebuke
> This drunkenness of triumph ere it die
> And dying, bring despair. Victory? poor slaves!

(928–30)

Now fully on the side of the poor Greek slaves who have, as dying captives, declared their belief in the ultimate triumph of thought, Mahmud goes out to quell the sense of triumph in his own forces – because he knows that the material victory has no reality, and because he sees that his forces are still 'poor slaves' to the concept of materialistic power. Perhaps he even hopes that he can, on the spot, bring them to see the truth that has just broken in on him. And this new truth of Mahmud's is not a vast or grand transcendental verity; it is the truth that, as Hoagwood perceives, underlies *Prometheus Unbound* as well as *Hellas*: that 'eternity is of *thought*, and thought is human and natural, not transcendental at all' (176).

The voices outside, however, continue to cry out 'Victory! Victory!' and they tell of Austrian, Russian, British, and French forces joining with the Turks in a frenzied alliance aimed at the total destruction of Greece. What the drama, though, has shown is that such tides of war have no ultimate reality if once the mind sets itself against them and the intellect assumes its rightful place as director of human affairs. In this assurance the Chorus ends the drama in a lyrical assertion:

The world's great age begins anew,
    The golden years return,
The earth doth like a snake renew
    Her winter weeds outworn;
Heaven smiles, and faiths and empires gleam
Like wrecks of a dissolving dream . . .

O, write no more the tale of Troy,
    If earth Death's scroll must be!
Nor mix with Laian rage the joy
    Which dawns upon the free;
Although a subtler Sphinx renew
Riddles of death Thebes never knew.

Another Athens shall arise,
    And to remoter time
Bequeath, like sunset to the skies,
    The splendour of its prime . . .
O cease! must hate and death return?
    Cease! must men kill and die?
Cease! drain not to its dregs the urn
    Of bitter prophecy.
The world is weary of the past,
O might it die or rest at last!

(1060–101)

The assertion is that if the past reliance on material power systems can finally be laid to rest, the world's great age, exemplified by the thought-based golden age of Greece, will return. People will then triumph by exchanging thoughts instead of blows. In his notes to *Hellas* (*Poetical Works*, 479–80), Shelley recognizes the risk he is taking in thus predicting 'a period of regeneration and happiness' but finds reassurance in his being, in this risk-taking, in the company of Isaiah and Virgil.

Hellas, then, serves as the culmination of Shelley's poetry of social enlightenment. That the poet in his prophetic, 'unacknowledged legislator' role must take the risks of true prophecy – must raise questions capable of unmasking historically-accumulated delusions – is primary in each of the poems dealt with in the present chapter. There is no doubt in Shelley's mind that if creative imagination is linked with an insistence upon intellectually honest, historically verifiable truth, the resultant effect for the betterment of thought and action in society will show the risk element itself to be essentially a delusion.

5

Comprehensiveness and Synthesis

Having dealt with various of Shelley's poems under three different emphases – intellect, love and social enlightenment – we come now to his artistic masterpiece *Prometheus Unbound* and to 'The Triumph of Life', the work which at the poet's early death was left unfinished. Though each work might well and fittingly have been considered under one of the above categories, and though a number of the works discussed in the earlier chapters achieve an approximate or equal degree of synthesis, it seems best to focus in this chapter on the notable manner in which both *Prometheus Unbound* and 'The Triumph of Life', each in its distinctive way, achieve a synthesis and comprehension of all three emphases. Whereas *Prometheus Unbound* dramatically presents the reunion of intellect and love as the agent of universal social enlightenment, 'The Triumph of Life', so far as its fragmentary state permits us to see, works toward a clarification of how much the mind must grasp and master if love is to be permitted its rightful place in social interactions.

In *Prometheus Unbound* Shelley's protagonist personifies the creative mind of mankind, the highest potentiality of the human intellect.[1] Yet, unmistakably, the horrible condition in which Prometheus finds himself, chained and tortured by Jupiter, is in its origin his own fault. He himself expressly identifies the source of Jupiter's power: 'I gave all/He has' (I.381–2). And Asia later verifies this assertion:

> Prometheus
> Gave wisdom, which is strength, to Jupiter
> And with this law alone: 'Let man be free,'
> Clothed him with the dominion of wide Heaven.
>
> (2.4.43–6)[2]

The fault of Prometheus lies in his not having retained the power and responsibility that rightfully belong to him. It is important that we keep in mind from the start the relationship of the human mind to the operation of Necessity in the universe. As already shown in our consideration of *Queen Mab*, Shelley thought of the human mind as prime mover, so far as human actions and events are concerned. From the basic direction or motivation of the mind follow in necessitarian certainty the causal successions of human experience. Not unlike the linkage in 'Mont Blanc' between the human mind and the mountain's 'silence and solitude' and certainly very similar to the mind's becoming the Wind itself in 'Ode to the West Wind', the role of free will, as represented in Prometheus, is of elemental importance in the determination of whether or not harmony with natural necessity can or will be achieved.

Since Jupiter has grossly violated the condition that specifies the freedom of mankind,[3] Prometheus has resisted him and has consequently endured ages of suffering as the chained captive of Jupiter. Not the least of his sufferings has been the knowledge that, if he would condone and aid Jupiter's usurpation of power, he could be free from torture. In his opening speech, Prometheus distinguishes carefully between the 'Mighty God' that Jupiter is and the 'Almighty' that he would have become had Prometheus 'deigned to share the shame' of the 'ill tyranny' that Jupiter has established (1.17–19). In this regard, Prometheus has been totally heroic in his suffering.

To the error of relinquishing to Jupiter any of his rightful responsibility, Prometheus, however, has added the egregious moral failure implicit in his response to being victimized by Jupiter; he has succumbed to respond in kind to Jupiter's vengefulness, has called down a horrendous curse upon Jupiter, and has been motivated by hatred through all the years of his endurance. His attitude toward Jupiter at the outset of the drama, a combination of defiant rage and sardonic disdain, is summed up in the line 'I laugh to scorn Jove's thunderbolt . . .', quoted not from *Prometheus Unbound* but from Euripides' satyr play *The Cyclops*, which, perhaps in mid-1819, Shelley translated in full.[4] Perceiving that the calculated designs of Jupiter have manifested themselves in a power principle applied by means of violence, Prometheus has himself adopted as his vengeful response to Jupiter's despotism a calculating power principle based on violence. Before he can be prepared to reanimate and preserve the imaginative creativity implicit in his reunion with Asia, Prometheus must recognize the need to destroy within himself the calculation-violence-power complex that has for so long motivated him. The essential symbolic significance of Shelley's poetic drama lies in the revolutionary process of regeneration that begins with the recognition of the essential identity of self-interested calculation and repressive violence – a process that culminates in the attainment of a viable humanity based on love.

The first step toward regeneration occurs as, suddenly in his first speech realizing the meaning of his error and his moral failure, Prometheus cries out that he no longer disdains but, instead, pities his arch enemy Jupiter (I.53).[5] Thus Prometheus, the moral and intellectual nature of mankind, the apex of human thought, dares to assume full responsibility for his decisions and actions and thereby to make possible the reattainment of his original or rightful condition: his being reunited with Asia, who is the spirit of all true beauty and love.

Prometheus declares himself to have been diametrically wrong in the values he has held since he first pronounced the curse. Coming to the realization that so long as he, the creative power of the human mind, does not reclaim and reassert his place of responsibility and dominance, Jupiter will hold mankind perpetually in pain and fear, Prometheus casts off his power-and-vengeance-oriented principles (ironically patterned after those of Jupiter) and accepts the exact opposite: the principle of love. The soul, the will, the imagination – whatever designation we give to the highest attribute of the human mind – makes this radical, revolutionary decision.[6] Thus Prometheus, who has been his own destroyer, becomes his own preserver as he acknowledges and assumes the power of love, the quality that can exist only in the original state of his union with Asia.

So long as he thinks vengefully of gaining power when he will be released, Prometheus, chained to the rock, is only a potential perpetuator of the destructive power cycles fostered by Jupiter. Not until he discards that motivation for a new orientation, in which he seeks only the creative reunion with Asia, does his life mean anything but the promise of another round of an old, unsatisfactory system. Emphatically, the drama shows that individuals, organizations, nations, and indeed humankind are deluded in their materialistic search for life by means of self-interested power and honour.

Shelley does not intend, however, to dictate direct applications to particular human situations or events. A genuine work of art, he believes, will provide the imaginative milieu in the context of which the reader will make the applications. He explains in the Preface that he intends his poetry to be free of didacticism, that it is directed toward that reader whose consciousness may recognize and respond to 'beautiful idealisms of moral excellence' (207) – the quality that he earlier has named 'Intellectual Beauty'. This quality, by the very fact of its disregard of all mundane systems of calculated self-interest, can lead the individual, and eventually mankind, to the one true life of actual love.

The extent to which the principle of self-preservation is ingrained in systems and individuals is emphasized at the end of the second act of *Prometheus Unbound*. Asia, singing of the journey to the realm of love, reveals metaphorically that it is a return journey, a discarding or a destruction of values accumulated in the various stages since birth. Imaginatively reversing the chronology of life – from age through mature adulthood, youth and infancy – she traces the concept of *being* 'Through Death and Birth, to a diviner day'. The equating of death and birth is especially important; it brings to a climax the revolutionary declaration in Asia's lines that nothing in the way of accrued values is inexpendable in the process of discovering love as the all-pervading value. Donald Reiman (*Percy Bysshe Shelley*, 81) correctly terms the last scene of Act 2, in which Asia sings this song, the 'keystone scene in the drama'. Appropriately placed at the structural centre of the drama, Asia's song may be called the heart or essence of this poetic work.

Saying so much for Asia's song is not meant to detract, however, from the importance of the action performed by Prometheus, especially what transpires in Act 1. Within the compass of the opening speech the crucial 'inner action' presents not only a crescendo of Prometheus' hate-filled resistance and plotting of revenge against the tyrant Jupiter, but also the initial, vital step of his journey toward a new life of love, a step that is simultaneous with his rejection of the hateful curse that has originated and symbolized his ages of bondage. Asia's song in Act 2 is a recapitulation and extension of the process initiated in the first speech of the drama.

With the cry, 'Ah no! I pity thee', Prometheus sets up a completely new basis for defiance of Jupiter. As the curse, upon his own request, is repeated to Prometheus, not only his own responsibility for Jupiter's power but also the depth and the recklessness of his blind hatred toward Jupiter are made evident. One portion of it reveals especially that the effects of a philosophy of vengeance and hatred are no more restricted in their scope and range than are (later) the effects of love as the principle of life:

> Ay, do thy worst. Thou art Omnipotent.
> O'er all things but thyself I gave thee power,
> And my own will. Be thy swift mischiefs sent
> To blast mankind, from yon ethereal tower.
> Let thy malignant spirit move
> In darkness over those I love:
> On me and mine I imprecate
> The utmost torture of thy hate . . .

> (1.272–9)

In this passage, by subjecting even 'those I love' to Jupiter's 'malignant spirit', the highest aspect of the human mind accepts the idea of tyranically imposed pain and subjugation as a part of the life of mankind. This is the Puritan–Calvinistic notion of fallen man in the vale of suffering and tears that constitutes earthly life.

What Prometheus, in his curse, has accepted is a frame of reference in which the problems of life can somehow be dealt with, though without a sense of human responsibility. 'In Romantic poems', says Jerome McGann, 'that frame of reference is precisely what stands at issue' (73). Though McGann's assertion is made in the context of his contrasting Blake's socially conscious poem 'London' with poems such as the more existentially accepting Medieval lyric 'Lullay, lullay, litel child', it is directly to the point with regard to what Prometheus rejects and what, instead, he accepts as he renounces the curse. In his curse, Prometheus gives the Byronic response to the notion of life's divinely-ordained trail of subjugation and agony – the response of resolute defiance despite the anticipated consequences.[7] Translated into terms of actual life, this means the suffering of countless individuals who are victims of power systems tolerated by a collective human mind that, though outraged, comprehends no alternative.

Having heard the entire curse repeated, Prometheus withdraws and renounces it as he cries out,

> It doth repent me: words are quick and vain;
> Grief for awhile is blind, and so was mine.
> I wish no living thing to suffer pain.

(1.303–5)

He does not forgive evil but asserts that to curse is merely negative;[8] it provides no way out of the old cycle. The blindness of his personified grief is an apt figure. We speak fittingly of blind rage and blind revenge; they are, if not morally acceptable, at least understandable reactions to certain outrageous events. Yet they *are* blind, and what their blindness hides is the very source of our essential humanity: the light of love. Prometheus has come to the realization that, if he is to find his way to the desired union with Asia and if they together are to bring about a truly new state of being, he must reject blind, cyclic retaliation and must walk in the path of love. One who loves has nothing to do with cursing or seeking revenge. On the path of love, of positive progression toward unity, this individual (or this human society) simply disregards the evil principle, leaving it to perish by the life-to-death cycle of which it is an integral part. Prometheus is, or course, not a whit closer to giving in; the desire that neither individual human beings nor even Jupiter should suffer pain is the outcome of the wholly new basis of his resistance to the principle of despotic power represented by Jupiter.

The fall of Jupiter does not occur until long after the crucial change has taken place in Prometheus. Indeed, the torture of Prometheus is in the interval intensified. While he continues to suffer, he knows that eventually the old cycle of evil will bring round the doom of Jupiter. As he tells Jupiter's lackey Mercury (1.422–7), the counting of the years may be the labour of what would seem to us an eternity. For Prometheus life no longer is a matter of calculating gain and loss, reward and retribution. As he calmly awaits the coming fall of Jupiter, he comments upon the old sense of justice (which he fully understands) and his newly-accepted concept of justice, which since it has nothing to do with retribution or revenge, is 'triumphant' in a way that staggers ordinary logic:

> Evil minds
> Change good to their own nature. I gave all
> He has, and in return he chains me here . . .

Whilst my beloved race is trampled down
By his thought-executing ministers.
Such is the tyrant's recompense: 'tis just:
He who is evil can receive no good . . .
Submission, thou dost know, I cannot try . . .
For justice when triumphant will weep down
Pity not punishment on her own wrongs,
Too much avenged by those who err.

(1.380–405)

Prometheus expresses here a profound insight with regard to rationalistic, retributive justice. He sees that it is oriented toward perpetuating the old or established way – rewarding compliance and punishing digression. Very perceptively, Shelley uses the image of Jupiter's bringing thought to trial, finding it guilty, and sentencing it to be executed. The irony of the image is profound; a system that declares thinking to be a crime has come to be known as justice, and who would dare oppose justice? Shelley sees little or no hope in the conventional system of justice for any significant departure from the established way. If the established way is evil, there is no hope for betterment in rationalistic justice. He who uses the evil establishment's own devices against that establishment, either sets up another system based on the same evil or is made the victim of the establishment's wrath. Even mere acquiescence in the evil establishment can bring only a 'just' confinement within its code.

Prometheus sees with equal keenness, on the other hand, into the *new* concept of justice. This 'triumphant' justice replaces punishment with pity, thus setting up a wholly new principle of life. Instead of calculating scores and seeking to even them, it ventures into the risks and the potentialities of continually becoming that which it idealizes. The radicalism in this new approach, in close accord with the theme of 'The Mask of Anarchy', is its quite clearly allowing for no participation in wars, executions, or assassinations – and for the presence of no prisons, no legal rights to more than equitable property, no social or racial class systems, no unfairly contrived political power blocks, nor any other personal or societal concepts that are based on the principle of calculation. To the extent that the serious reader is sympathetic with Prometheus as

Act 1 progresses, he or she must find virtually all of established society perverted to an alarming extent.

The Chorus of Furies, in the course of the intensified torture of Prometheus, sets before him visions of past efforts to bring about the revolution he desires, all of which have failed dismally. The prime example is the movement initiated and inspired by Jesus Christ (1.546–59); and any so-called 'Christian' nation of the twentieth century, confronted with the multiple, threatening prospects of environmental pollution, internal rebellion of the disadvantaged and an ultimate world war, might be said to serve as a lingering case in point for the torturing furies.

When one of the Furies, in a last effort to achieve the capitulation of Prometheus, flashes before him a vision of Christ on the cross, Prometheus, though touched with agonizing pity, refuses to speak the name of Christ because 'It hath become a curse'. The tragically ironic outcome of Christ's mission to humanity is voiced as Prometheus declares,

> I see
> The wise, the mild, the lofty and the just,
> Whom thy slaves hate for being like to thee,
> . . . kneaded down in common blood . . . .

> (1.604–14)

Those who slavishly follow a *form* of Christianity are thus seen to turn most viciously on those who *in fact* follow the teachings of Christ. The Fury responds by listing the ways in which good intentions have become confused with evil – how fear, truth, timidity, power, wisdom and love have become jumbled, meaningless terms – all because hypocrisy and custom have made human existence static and dead rather than vital and evolving. The most tragic irony is that, not daring to 'devise good for man's estate', the 'loftiest' yet 'know not that they do not dare' (1.619–24). This is the same condition described by William Butler Yeats in the opening lines of 'The Second Coming' – the falling-apart that is succeeded by an unknown manner of being, threatening these of the status quo. What Prometheus comes to realize is that he, the apex of the human mind, will determine what the new manner of being advocated by Christ will be and that his must be the courage to see it through to actualization. When he, then, applies his newly accepted justice of pity – 'Thy words are like a cloud of winged snakes / Any yet, I pity those they torture not' – the Fury gives up in dismay and vanishes.

Prometheus, it must be emphasized, is not for Shelley a god in the sense of being a power outside mankind or outside the individual; he is, rather, the creativity latent within a person and within society (that is to say, within the imaginative mind), needing for his liberation and reunion with Asia only the stamina of steadfast will. Truly imaginative creativity in any and all areas can translate existence from the distorted deathliness described by the fury into genuine life or immortality.

When, after the victory over the Furies' torments, Prometheus is encouraged by ministering spirits, one of them assures him that from 'shapes that haunt thought's wildernesses', the poet can create 'Forms more real than living man, / Nurslings of immortality!' (1.748–9). And Prometheus accepts that reality – not the mundane, materialistic values that have distorted or obliterated 'living man' – as the operative principle for the attainment of meaning in life. When he declares, 'Most vain all hope but love' (1.808), he means that mere pity is not enough, that nothing equals love in bringing about imaginative progression. The positive, progressive element is in his reunification with love, which must command all his dedication and effort. If strong enough, he, the highest form of human intellect, will attain reunion with Asia, the noblest expression of love, imaginative creation and beauty. Both will die to their former isolated selves and, united in new life, will be able to save humanity from the recurring cycle of vengeful hatred. Prometheus, if he cannot live in this unifying truth of love, will choose obliteration:

> I would fain
> Be what it is my destiny to be,
> The saviour and the strength of suffering man,
> Or sink into the original gulf of things.

> (1.815–18)

The mind, in other words, has a mission through its capacity for imaginative, loving identification to elevate and renew human society.

On this note of belief in 'forms more real than living man' the first act ends, leaving Prometheus as firmly bound and severely tortured as at the opening of the drama. He is within himself, however, already newly alive in the self-annihilating love that will become fruitful when Jupiter falls – instead of death-bound in the self-preserving hate and vengeance that would merely have set up another regime like Jupiter's.

In Act 2 the scene shifts to a vale in the Caucasian Mountains, where Asia, in her separation from Prometheus, is reunited with Panthea and Ione, her two sisters, and all three prepare for the release of Prometheus. Asia, a character of Shelley's invention, replaces the more generalized and less impressive Oceanides of Aeschylus' drama and thus, in Webb's view, provides one of the most notable ways in which Shelley's story differs from that of Aeschylus (210). The emphasis throughout the act is on the universal unity that is waiting to be symbolized as well as instigated by the reunion of Prometheus and Asia. Panthea, while with Ione tending Prometheus sympathetically in his torture, has had two dreams, one of which she recalls and narrates to Asia (2.1.71–106). Without reserve or reticence about her dream's transcendence of conventional restraints, Ione expresses symbolically as well as literally Shelley's conviction that when once the collective human mind will have replaced the principle of retaliation with the principle of love, the action of this new urge will penetrate, barrier after barrier, into succeeding selfhoods to erase greed, jealousy, and egoism so as to form an essential unity in which diverse elements are not crushed but intermingled in continual creative contact. The infinity of the process is well expressed in the continuing conversation of the sisters, as Asia, looking into Panthea's eyes, sees there the second dream, which is really Prometheus' vision sent by him. As Hoagwood makes clear, it is also Panthea's vision, 'because it appears in her eyes; and yet it is Asia's because she reads it and casts it in language. The three figures are, therefore, united by this vision' (160). Reading the dream in Panthea's eyes, Asia feels herself drawn into the whole universe of sky and orbs as she comes to realize that it is not her own reflection but really the vision of Prometheus that is reflected back to her in Panthea's eyes:

> *Asia.* There is a change: beyond their inmost depth
> I see a shade – a shape – 'tis He, arrayed
> In the soft light of his own smiles which spread

Like radiance from the cloud-surrounded moon.
Prometheus, it is thou.

(2.1.119–23)

Without any trace of conventional or generally expected jealousy,
Asia, spouse or mate of Prometheus, responds thus lovingly to
the loving presence of Prometheus in Panthea's mind, thus providing an instance of the infinite yet undiminishing divisibility of
love that Shelley seeks to clarify in 'Epipsychidion'.
Love is the universal force of continual and contagious perfectibi-
lity. It has nothing to do with calculating profit and loss, with
required giving and taking. Love is, in fact, as Demogorgon
declares to Asia, the 'deep truth' that is 'imageless' (2.4.116) in the
sense of being realizable not through any artificial forms but only
through experience. It is the one force available to the mind that is
entirely free and infinitely superior to all that enslaves or is
enslaved.[9] And what Demogorgon reveals to Asia has to be
convincing because the process of her dialogue with him is really
a mental one – within her own consciousness. Making the point that
one's definition of Demogorgon depends upon one's perception of
him, that he is perceived as destroyer only by those who oppose
the process of temporal change, Cronin (157) quotes from Mary
Wollstonecraft's earlier description of this amorphous Miltonic
character as 'the shapeless void of eternity – For shape can it be
called that shape hath none?' Hoagwood, asserting that Demogorgon is 'located within the human mind', declares perceptively that
Asia's transfiguration and Prometheus' liberation are not due to
the operation of an external agent but that they are occasioned by
the unveiling of a mental power from within. 'What Asia discovers',
says Hoagwood, 'is no transcending deity of the sort that she
thought she should worship; she discovers the power of her mind'
(168–9). Asia thus finds within herself the evidence of the 'deep
truth' of love that alone is free from all subjection and that
Prometheus has found and put into practice in Act 1.

Asia is herself the embodiment or personification of imaginative
beauty's, or love's, potentiality. As Woodring explains, she is 'a
ray of what man can know as the eternal One, . . . love, beauty,
and light . . . : Shelley calls her love; if you know of something
better than love, Asia will be that something for you. To thought
she is warmth' (284). As personification of that which can make

human thought the germinating agent of moral growth in society, Asia explains before bursting into song that a confrontation between individuals who truly love is not a matter of the giver's being deprived and the receiver's obtaining the benefit. Rather, to inspire love and to feel it are both fortunate or happy experiences:

> . . . All love is sweet,
> Given or returned; common as light is love
> And its familar voice wearies not ever . . .
> They who inspire it most are fortunate
> As I am now; but those who feel it most
> Are happier still, after long sufferings
> As I shall soon become.

(2.5.39–47)

Having presented the entirely positive responses of Asia, Panthea, and Ione to the transition from hate to love that is made in Act 1 by Prometheus, Act 2 concludes with Asia's song (already discussed) which suggests that the two fragmentary beings, Prometheus and Asia, have indeed travelled backward through existence, through death and birth, into the true existence which is individual consciousness and are now prepared for their new, united wholeness of being.

Act 3, telling of the fall of Jupiter and the actual release of Prometheus, shows the glorious results of the transformation that has taken place. The act opens, by way of contrast, with a highly satirical and ironic parody of the unified, creative life. Believing that his copulation with Thetis has engendered an expected son who will perpetuate his tyranny, Jupiter ironically declares her to have been made one with him and exults in the memory of that copulation (3.1.37–49). Earl Wasserman (*Shelley's Prometheus Unbound*, 90) has aptly said of this union of Jupiter and Thetis that it 'is not, as Jupiter believes, a fertile mingling of "Two mighty spirits" productive of a third; it is a sterile rape, . . . a gruesome parody of the love-union of Prometheus and Asia'. In terms of life as we experience it, this means that in a system based on the power principle and on materialistic calculation of profit and loss, true creativity – true art or a genuine perfecting of humanity – is only an illusion.

The fall of Jupiter occurs as Demogorgon, relentless destiny, compels Jupiter to follow him 'down the abyss' (3.1.53), which, as Cronin explains (156), is actually the same abyss into which Asia and Panthea had descended. Cronin further perceives it to be in effect the same cave into which Prometheus and Asia retire. The difference lies in Jupiter's perceiving it as a hell and Prometheus and Asia's perceiving it as a pastoral retreat. Jupiter's view of the change as defeat for his regime and victory for a new tyrannical regime contrasts diametrically with Prometheus and Asia's disregard for such self-interested calculation and with their acceptance of the essential freedom of the human mind, even from subjection to the godhead that Prometheus and Asia themselves represent. With this trust in humanity as their essential victory, they are free to retire from the system of cyclic despotism. Having, by the respective self-annihilations of their union, removed from the world of actual human affairs the threat of domination by their godhead, they may, of course, retire and be a mere though invaluably precious point of reference in the cave of the human skull.

Before their retreat to the haven of their cave, Prometheus speaks of on-going new forms to be produced in the eternal springtime of his union with Asia:

> And lovely apparitions dim at first
> Then radiant – as the mind, arising bright
> From the embrace of beauty . . .
> casts on them
> The gathered rays which are reality –
> Shall visit us, the progeny immortal
> Of Painting, Sculpture and rapt Poesy,
> And arts, though unimagined, yet to be.

(3.3.49–56)

Implicit in this declaration about the art of the new reality is the essential correlation between art and life; and this being so, the 'becoming' that is life is an attribute also of art to the extent that there are 'arts, though unimagined, yet to be'.

For old arts to die and new ones to be born, there must, then, be a radical change in what constitutes life – an equal acceptance of coming and of going. Earth, the giver and taker of physical life, tells Asia and Prometheus of her attitude toward life and death in the new era:

> And death shall be the last embrace of her
> Who takes the life she gave, even as a mother
> Folding her child, says, 'Leave me not again!'

> (3.3.105–7)

Earth takes this opportunity to explain the distinction between the spirit that is Asia (which can become one with the highest level of the human mind) and the traditionally accepted limitation that is called mortality:

> Thou art immortal and this tongue is known
> But to the uncommunicating dead. –
> Death is the veil which those who live call life:
> They sleep – and it is lifted.

> (3.3.111–14)

Here Shelley expresses the same idea as that of the 'dome of many coloured glass' passage in *Adonais*. As is true of that passage,[10] the meaning of Earth's speech is at best evasive unless we see that the two words *death* and *life* must not merely exchange definitions but must each take on a *different* meaning. When she calls it a 'veil which those who live call life', Earth is not defining *death* as we use the term. Rather, she is saying that in the distorted realm of Jupiter, to live (*exist* seems intended here) in the belief that life is the getting and maintaining of power, honour and material goods, is really to experience death, not life. For those who thus exist, true life is made apparent only when they sleep and the veil is lifted in dreams. Then they can experience truth such as Panthea and Ione experienced in their sleep, the truth of the oneness of all beings. But as the Jupiter-deluded mortals awaken, the truth of genuinely imaginative life seems totally unreal and they accept again the veil of death (separateness, egoistic striving, etc.) which they call reality or life.

Shelley's 1818 sonnet 'Lift not the painted veil . . .' contains the same idea of life as only a veil. The unnamed character in the sonnet, however, who is said to have lifted the veil, appears to be not Promethean but, rather, comparable to the young Poet of *Alastor*. Moving among the 'unheeding many' as a 'splendour among shadows', he, like the *Alastor* poet, strives for truth but does not find it. Merely to lift the veil, seeking for 'things to love' leads only to a confrontation of both Hope and Fear, who cancel each other and leave the seeker totally disoriented in an existence that is known to be not really life. Prometheus and Asia, however, are leading humanity out of that world of illusion; the veil is being entirely torn away. They will from this time forth permit people to live in the unity of the eternal moment in which evolving truth is perpetually and directly confronted, a realm where falsehood ceases because there is no evil of death (falsely called life) upon which hope and fear can weave distorted images.

The only hope, then, lies in annihilating this veil of death in self-annihilation. As life is thus transformed to the immortal realm of Prometheus, death will have lost its power, for it is not real at all (in the conventional sense) in a world where each is all and all are each. It is to a higher level of insight such as this that Shelley wishes, as he states in the Preface, to raise the consciousness of his readers. The difficulty of his task becomes apparent when after a study of *Prometheus Unbound* we find ourselves, despite what truth we may have found in it, still talking to our associates in the 'real' world in terms of 'real' things such as power politics, the national interest, economic theories, property rights and personal advancement.

In the fourth scene of Act 3 the transformation of humankind is described in terms of the shedding of old, ugly shapes and visages. Men abandon, among other 'foul masks', their 'dull sneer of self-loved ignorance' (3.4.43); women, 'looking emotions once they feared to feel', are 'changed to all which once they dared not be' (3.4.158–9). The Promethean transformation is the realization of that to which the poet has dedicated himself in 'Hymn to Intellectual Beauty'; *both* self-love *and* self-contempt are gone (3.4.174–9). With the description, at the close of Act 3, of a universal benign anarchy, Shelley clearly points out the extent of the mental revolution that he considers necessary for the liberation of humanity. No nationalism, no social or economic class, and no religious dogma remain. People retain passions, it is true, but not a helpless submission to them. The passions now serve humanity, as do also chance, death and mutability.[11] The point is that when self-centredness disappears, with it disappear all those aspects of societal and individual life that have formerly made human beings their slaves.[12] Though ruling them like slaves, people are also still subject to the influence of 'chance, death, and mutability'. Webb suggests that this sobering note on the human need for goals yet to be attained may have been Shelley's response to the somewhat too simple view of Godwin, Condorcet and others regarding human perfectability (118). The act ends not with an escapist dream of unattainable perfection but with the realization that Prometheus' triumph has won for people the ability to attain true humanity through liberated thought.

Some months after completing Act 3, having in the interval composed *The Cenci*, Shelley had a new burst of inspiration and added, as Act 4, a grand concluding hymn of praise and triumph honouring the union of Prometheus and Asia, the symbolic liberation of humanity. Having in various ways throughout the drama made attempts to convey the unity in action and interaction that constitutes the 'mighty motion' of the many in one and the one in the many, he finally is most successful in the passage in which Panthea tells of her vision of a sphere composed of intermingling spheres:

> And from the other opening in the wood
> Rushes with loud and whirlwind harmony
> A sphere, which is as many thousand spheres,
> Solid as crystal, yet through all its mass
> Flow, as through empty space, music and light:
> Ten thousand orbs involving and involved,
> Purple and azure, white and green and golden,
> Sphere within sphere, and every space between
> Peopled with unimaginable shapes
> Such as ghosts dream dwell in the lampless deep
> Yet each intertranspicuous, and they whirl
> Over each other with a thousand motions
> Upon a thousand sightless axles spinning
> And with the force of self-destroying swiftness,
> Intensely, slowly, solemnly roll on.

> (4.236–50)

Panthea goes on to tell how, cradled as a smiling child within the orb, Earth's spirit projects from its forehead 'Vast beams' that flash backward through history on Earth's cycles to prehistoric times and reveal that these cycles simply are no more (4.270–318).[13] Light emanating from the forehead to transcend history, particularly as it combines with the imagery of childhood's potentiality, is one of Shelley's most successful images of the human mind's capacity to be 'King of Life' and to bring human society back into harmony with the natural spheres of the universe. The entire scene of the orb and the beams of light correlates well with the action and symbolism of the first three acts; it represents and amplifies the vision for which Prometheus has endured torture, the dreams of Panthea and Asia, Asia's song of the return 'Through Death and Birth, to a diviner day', and the scene of mankind's discarding its age-old ugly forms in favour of a new state of being.

Earth sings a song of contrast. She recalls how Jupiter, the 'Sceptered Curse', has threatened to 'splinter and knead down my children's bones, / All I bring forth, to one void mass battering and blending', until all the works of nature and all human beings should be 'stamped by the strong hate into a lifeless mire' (4.338–49). The contrast with the orb's harmony that has just been so powerfully presented is consciously and emphatically intended. But Earth immediately begins to rejoice in Jupiter's vanishing into nothing and in love's filling the void and darkness left by his disappearance.

> How art thou sunk, withdrawn, cover'd – drunk up
> By thirsty nothing, as the brackish cup
> Drained by a Desart-troop – a little drop for all;
> And from beneath, around, within, above,
> Filling thy void annihilation, Love
> Bursts in like light on caves cloven by the thunderball.
>
> (4.350–5)

Further to emphasize the contrast between Jupiter's tendency to batter people into 'one void mass' and the oneness brought about by Prometheus, Earth sings in a later song:

> Man, oh, not men! a chain of linked thought,
> Of love and might to be divided not . . .
>
> Man, one harmonious Soul of many a soul
> Whose nature is its own divine controul . . .
>
> (4.394–401)

Finally Demogorgon, the spirit of natural and infinite potential-ity,[14] addresses Man, to whom he asserts the values of 'Gentleness, Virtue, Wisdom and Endurance' (4.562) that prevail in the new springtime of unity; he urges that if ever despotism should regain the upper hand, these values or powers be again applied in order to bring in another new age of love. In conclusion, Demogorgon declares profoundly that nothing less than an unwavering, cre-atively imaginative concept of suffering, forgiveness, defiance of power, love, endurance and hope can make humanity 'Good, great and joyous, beautiful and free' – that 'This is alone Life, Joy, Empire and Victory'.

To the awful conditions that threaten to annihilate humankind – militarism, poverty, environmental pollution, over-population – the 'beautiful idealisms of moral excellence' so profoundly portrayed in *Prometheus Unbound* might yet be applied. To the extent that this application is not being made, Prometheus, the highest aspect of the human mind, has not in actuality dared to re-assume the rightful responsibility that ages ago he abdicated to Jupiter, the abstract principle of conformity and ego-gratifying power. Shelley perceived clearly that only as he becomes the actual destroyer of Jupiter's power, not by conventional might but, rather, by the imaginative method of nonviolently asserting a truly creative and positive way of life, will Prometheus be able to be (as he rightfully should be) the preserver of humanity.

'The Triumph of Life', left in a fragmentary condition at Shelley's death, is too easily taken as a work indicating the poet's disillusion-ment with the essence of what his previous poetry had built up, especially as it had attained a culmination in *Prometheus Unbound*. Admittedly, 'The Triumph of Life' is not conclusive and comes, at the end of its extant portion, to the utterance of the frustrated question, 'Then what is life?' How Shelley would have dealt with an answer or with possible answers to that question must remain largely conjectural.

We do, however, have suggestions in the poem that its con-clusion would in all likelihood not have been as dismal and deterministically forlorn as some critics have surmised.[15] As in earlier works, there are indications in 'The Triumph of Life' that Shelley has not wavered in his strong assurance that true life consists in the mind's uniting with love, thus to deal creatively with experience. Foremost among these is the imagery of night and stars that forms a contrast and a welcome alternative to the painfully piercing brightness of the daylight that hides the stars and ushers in the time of the subjugating chariot.

> But I, whom thoughts which must remain untold
>
> > Had kept as wakeful as the stars that gem
> > The cone of night, now they were laid asleep,
> > Stretched my faint limbs beneath the hoary stem
>
> > Which an old chestnut flung athwart the steep
> > Of a green Apennine: before me fled
> > The night; behind me rose the day . . .

> (21–7)

His back to the rising day, his thoughts having kept him wakefully alert as are the stars at night, the narrator, much as does the speaker in Blake's 'Mad Song', turns his face to the night.[16] Thus there is at the poem's outset a strong suggestion that the brightness of daylight's vision may but present us with a dream image of apparently even more dazzling brightness while blinding us to the specific, particular and beautiful truths of life that, one by one, the symbolic stars can reveal to perceptive thought. Both 'The Sensitive Plant' and the conclusion of *Adonais*, in their star imagery, provide parallels to this passage. Nevertheless, because 'The Triumph of Life' remains fragmentary, such indications in this poem are less conclusive than those in the other poems.

As the narrator tells of his early-morning waking dream, we learn that in it he has seen vast multitudes of human beings all moving rapidly along a barren, dusty stretch of ground in various attitudes of fear, involvement with the fears of others, mournful contemplation and gloomy dread of death. But most importantly, they

> Pursued or shunned the shadows the clouds threw
> Or birds within the noonday ether lost,
>
> Upon that path where flowers never grew;
> And weary with vain toil and faint for thirst
> Heard not the fountains whose melodious dew

> Out of their mossy cells forever burst
> Nor felt the breeze which from the forest told
> Of grassy paths, and wood-lawns interspersed
> With overarching elms and caverns cold,
> And violet banks where sweet dreams brood, but they
> Pursued their serious folly as of old . . .

(63–73)

That it is folly and that they pursue it indicates that these multitudes are blameworthy. The barren, dusty tract is not the only world available to them; the sound of the fountains and the sensations imparted by the breeze tell as much. Had the individuals willed to do so, they could, it seems, have found the pleasant life symbolized by the images of dew, moss, grassy paths, wood-lawns, elms, cold caverns and violet-covered banks. The narrator says that they *did* not hear and *did* not feel – not that they *could* not hear and feel – respectively, the fountain and the breeze.

Having, in his waking dream seen the multitude pervert the forms of dance and song (universal symbols of freedom and creativity) to the expression of their abject enslavement to the chariot of life that rolls over them, the narrator has come to realize that the only ones who ever had escaped domination by the chariot were

> . . . the sacred few who could not tame
> Their spirits to the Conqueror, but as soon
> As they had touched the world with living flame
>
> Fled back like eagles to their native noon,
> Or those who put aside the diadem
> Of earthly thrones or gems . . .

(128–33)

Mentioning Athens and Jerusalem, the narrator seems to have in mind Socrates and Christ as outstanding examples of the very few whose spirits – powers of mind and volition – were strong enough not to be tamed to the otherwise universal submission, who could resist the temptations of power and wealth.

That the chariot itself is a mental construct that has power only in the mind is suggested by the narrator's telling that, after its sudden disappearance ('Yet ere I can say *where* – the chariot hath/Passed over them' [161–2]), the only trace in nature that he is able to find is 'as of foam after the Ocean's wrath/Is spent upon the desert shore' (163–4). The chariot's one continuing effect is on the multitude of people, who, 'not the less with impotence of will' (170) continue their ghastly dance until they drop and die. The important point is that their will is impotent, apparently mesmerized by what only *seems* to be reality.

In the aftermath of this dream, the narrator discovers nearby upon the ground, apparently left behind by the dream's pageant, the remaining incorporation of what was once Rousseau, who takes on the role of interpreter and guide for him and tells him that the chariot he has seen is indeed 'Life' (180). But whatever Rousseau may mean by the term, we need to recognize that it is only what people *call* life (as in *Prometheus Unbound*, 'the veil which those who live call life').[17] Rousseau declares that, if the narrator can 'forbear/To join the dance, which I had well forborne', he will 'tell all that which to this deep scorn/Led me and my companions' (188–92). Thus he clearly indicts himself along with the other captives of the chariot for not having trusted the strength of their human ability to think. To the narrator's asking, 'And who are those chained to the car?' he replies that they are the wise, great and unforgotten,

> . . . they who wore
> Mitres and helms and crowns, or wreaths of light,
> Signs of thought's empire over thought; their lore
>
> Taught them not this – to know themselves; their
>   might
> Could not repress the mutiny within,
>   And for the morn of truth they feigned, deep night
> Caught them ere evening.
>
> (208–15)

Had these illustrious personages of history followed the injunction of Socrates, they would have known that merely to feign the truth, merely to give the outward appearance of being in charge of the will, leads soon to darkness. As Rousseau's words suggest, the 'mutiny within' has subdued the potential power of their thought to direct them to the actual morning of the light of truth that could have led humanity onward. Instead, by a feigned attainment of the 'morn of truth', humanity has been caught in 'deep night'.

Rousseau's own sad state is evident in his having kept his mind just keen enough to maintain a degree of knowledge of himself and of how he has come to be what he is:

> Whence I came, partly I seem to know,
>
> And how and by what paths I have been brought
>   To this dread pass, methinks even thou mayst
>   guess;
> Why this should be my mind can compass not;
>
> Whither the conqueror hurries me still less.

                          (300–4)

Described in the poem as having merely holes where his eyes had been (187–8), this sightless Rousseau does, however, clearly recall a dream vision similar to the narrator's, beginning in Rousseau's case with the appearance of a female 'Shape all light' (352), who, in her outshining of the sun, appears to be a false light blinding him to the real truth.

> And still her feet, no less than the sweet tune
>   To which they moved, seemed as they moved, to blot
>   The thoughts of him who gazed on them, and soon
>
> All that was seemed as if it has been not,
>   As if the gazer's mind was strewn beneath
> Her feet like embers, and she, thought by thought.
>
> Trampled its fires into the dust of death . . .

                          (382–8)

Though to some extent parallel to the dream vision experienced by the young Poet of *Alastor*, this 'Shape all light' is seen as essentially negative in both its purpose and effect – whereas the *Alastor* vision is negative only in its effect, and that is only because the young Poet misinterprets its purpose. In the presentation of the 'Shape all light' the imagery of trampling, of dying embers and of blotted thought is overwhelmingly negative. Even the simile of this light's being like the coming day that 'Treads out the lamps of night' until the return of evening 'reillumines even the least / Of heaven's living eyes' (390–2) draws our sympathy toward the beautiful, thought-spark stars at night, rather than toward the light that by its very brightness obliterates these stars.[18]

To this thought-destroyer Rousseau addresses his plea for meaning, and she offers a cup from which to drink. Consistent with her trampling of thought is the effect of the potion that is in the cup:

> I rose; and, bending at her sweet command,
>   Touched with faint lips the cup she raised,
> And suddenly my brain became as sand
>
>   Where the first wave had more than half erased
> The track of deer on desert Labrador.
>
> (403–7)

The vision of the exceedingly bright chariot then appears to Rousseau, and in its dazzling light the Shape herself becomes a faded, glimmering figure of diminished light,[19] keeping her 'obscure tenour . . . / Beside my path, as silent as a ghost' (432–3), escorting him dimly, keeping him in the realm of false life. It is in this realm that the chariot, the same as in the narrator's vision, has first appeared to Rousseau. He is swept along. Still conscious of the truth, which in a parenthetical reference he rightly attributes to Dante, that 'all things are transfigured except Love' (476) but that this is beyond the comprehension of the thought-trampled world into which he has been seduced, Rousseau tells the narrator at some length of the phantoms, shadows and other horrid shapes that peopled his chariot-ridden, dream-vision world. Some of these distorted beings, he says, have finally died; others have fallen, as he has, tired of the dance. It is at this point that the narrator cries out, 'Then what is life?'

The ambiguity at this fragmentary leaving-off point is, at least apparently, very thick. Rousseau has told of the thoughtless condition in which he in his dream vision has seen the chariot and has been drawn into its sphere of domination. How, we ask, can we be expected to take seriously any reality revealed to one whose thoughts have been trampled into dust and even further obscured by a thought-dimming potion – and in a mere dream, at that? But here is Rousseau himself, left over from that dream, beside the narrator in the poem, the narrator himself having just come out of a dream-vision into waking consciousness. Or *is* he actually awake and conscious? If the whole poem represents a dream-state, then the presence of Rousseau makes sense; if not, then the narrator's waking reality must be flawed. In all this ambiguity, the reader must evaluate Rousseau's declaration that the chariot is 'Life'. What kind of guide to meaning is this victim of a dream-vision trampling and drugging of the brain? And that this should have happened to the poet Rousseau, for whom Shelley had great respect and fondness, does not diminish the deep puzzlement.

I shall resist the temptation to guess or conjecture how Shelley would have resolved this vast ambiguity. The achievement of the fragment as it stands amply reassures us that Shelley has not deserted, or been deserted by, the truth of the mind's creative responsibility that is so strongly asserted in *Prometheus Unbound*. One thing about which we can be quite clear is that Rousseau's identifying the chariot as 'Life' is not reliable. The chariot may be only the false appearances and values that have taken on the appearance of life. This being so, we may turn to the narrator, whose mind is still whole and untrampled, to see how far he can proceed in finding an answer for himself. Since the poem, however, is left a fragment, we can find there no conclusive answer or solution but must turn to our own minds, which, as Shelley's earlier poetry has variously shown us, must, taking into account both love and social needs, themselves confront the issue.

And that, finally, is the comprehensive theme in all of Shelley's great poetry: that the responsibility lies within us, in our minds, which when unfettered *can* discern what is true. Essential confrontation of an issue or a concept, he is certain, comes about through imagination, and that is the business of poetry – of any act of creative endeavour. What this poetic insight enables us to achieve is, in the words of the *Defence of Poetry*, 'to imagine that which we know' (502), which means to accept and act upon that which, on the basis of *all* the tests of the fully engaged mind, we find to be personally and convincingly true.

The only guide we have is love, the imageless certainty that others matter as much as we do and that to act for and in concert with them is to find the true self. If, with Prometheus, we genuinely 'wish no living thing to suffer pain', we find all the combined beauty and truth that (to borrow from Keats's very Shelleyan concept) is all we know on earth and all we need to know.

Notes

CHAPTER 1: INTRODUCTION

1. The problem in White's essay is mainly that he equates revolution with violent action, thus neglecting the creativity of Shelley's thought regarding the possibility of nonviolent revolution.
2. Webb (208). For a discussion of Shelley's view of Greece as his favourite country of the mind, see Webb's chapter 'The Greek Example' (191–227).
3. William Keach (16, 22, 33, 46, 199–200) deals with the influence that thinkers such as Bacon, Drummond, Hume and Locke had on Shelley's concept of language. Richard Cronin (1, 13–14, 77–83) relates Shelley's thought to that of Locke and Hume.
4. See *Shelley's Poetry and Prose* (482–3). Unless otherwise indicated, all references to Shelley's works pertain to this edition. Parenthetical references to prose works are by page numbers; parenthetical references to poetry are by line numbers.
5. Brown (367), defines prophecy as 'a critical response to the "urban revolution", that irreversible commitment of the human race to the city and civilization which spread outward from the "Nile to Oxus" heartland beginning around 3000 B.C. Prophecy is the perception of the potentialities, both for "good" and for "evil", inherent in the new social structure.'
6. Woodring (305) comments: 'A poet can show infallibly what spirit of events is possible. He foreknows because he perceives the present truly and fully. . . . The poet knows through imagination the means to moral regeneration.'
7. On pp. 76–88 Dawson traces some important influences of Godwin upon Shelley and some of Shelley's anticipations and extensions of, as well as exceptions to, Godwin's ideas.
8. For commentary on Hazlitt's later unjust denunciation of Shelley as reformer, see Dawson (187).
9. See Dawson (7).
10. See Reiman, *Percy Bysshe Shelley* (3).

CHAPTER 2: THE EMPHASIS ON INTELLECT

1. See *Shelley's Prose* (174n).
2. Among early evaluative comments on the Scrope Davies papers, which contain manuscripts by Byron as well as by Shelley, is Hymes's assertion that 'the importance of the documents . . . lies more in their commercial value . . . than in anything they add to our knowledge or

estimation of the two poets'. Holmes, 'Scrope's Last Throw', finds the papers more valuable because of the new material they present, but his focus is more on their contribution to a new public interest in the vacillating fortunes of Scrope Davies than on an evaluation of the poems they contain.

3. Rogers (3), suggests that the two sonnets to some extent foreshadow the mood of 'Hymn to Intellectual Beauty' and 'Mont Blanc'. Chernaik and Burnett (41), also touch upon the two sonnets' compatibility with the two longer poems.

4. Mr Christopher Norman-Butler of Barclays Bank, Ltd., London, has kindly given me permission to use, for this study, the sonnets and portions of the other two poems of the notebook.

5. The title given it in the notebook is not 'Mont Blanc' but 'Scene – Mont Pellisier in the Vale of Servoz'. (In the Bodleian MS Shelley adds e 16 p 3, it reads: 'At Pont Pellisier' revised to 'The scene of Pont Pellisier, at the extremity of the vale of Servoz'.)

6. McNiece, 'Poet as Ironist' (320–2), presents a perceptive discussion of this line. See particularly his assertion, 'Nature and mind ought not to be linked or "reconciled" as in religious faith'. For a contrary view see Chernaik, *Lyrics* (59n). Chernaik's discussion of both 'Mont Blanc' and 'Hymn to Intellectual Beauty' is insightful and rewarding. I intend here to express a difference of opinion only with regard to her interpretation of the one line.

7. The Bodleian MS, in which portions (because of numerous cancellations) are particularly difficult to read, contains in this passage a cancelled word that appears to be *mast*, a column or pillar on a ship.

8. A distinction made by Rieder seems apropos here. He asserts that, 'Unlike Shelley's authority, which is a moment, Coleridge's is a monument' (778). I take this to mean that, not accepting or needing the Coleridgean emphasis on past certitudes and established belief, Shelley finds support in the processes of moments in the world of natural necessity – the world with which people's minds need to be reunited.

9. See Coleridge, *Selected Poetry and Prose* (15). Subsequent reference to Coleridge's poetry is made by line reference and pertains to this edition.

10. These are excerpts from lines 816–21 of the projected long poem 'The Recluse' (1.1). The 107-line passage of which they are a part was first published in 1814 at the end of Wordsworth's Preface to *The Excursion*. See Wordsworth, *Selected Poems and Prefaces* (46). Subsequent reference to Wordsworth's poetry is made by line reference and pertains to this edition.

11. That Shelley meant the line specifically to designate established Christian doctrine is shown by variants in the Davies manuscript that agree with and confirm as intended the wording in the Bodleian manuscript and that corroborate a correction, in Shelley's hand, in the copy of the poem (clipped from the *Examiner* of 19 January 1817, where it was first published) that is included in the Shelley notebook at Harvard University. Curran, 'Shelley's Emendations', and Chernaik,

'Textual Emandations', both deal with corrections that Shelley made on the Harvard notebook copy of the 'Hymn'. The Reiman and Powers edition adopts Shelley's correction of the *Examiner* clipping.

12. In the simile of Intellectual Beauty's nourishing thought as darkness nourishes a dying flame (44–5), Shelley presents a complicated image. Reiman and Powers (*Shelley's Poetry and Prose*, 94n) suggest that, as darkness does not literally provide fuel for the flame, so Intellectual Beauty is not to be seen as a supplier of food for thought but rather as a kind of antithetical foil to set it off. Darkness may also be said to nourish a flame by providing for it a milieu in which to function with purpose – thus giving it meaning. It is in the latter sense that the concept of nourishment looks ahead to the image of the water-supplying 'source of human thought' in line 5 of 'Mont Blanc'.

13. Since the fourth stanza is not included in the Bodleian manuscript, only the two versions are available for comparison.

14. The shadow or shade imagery is considerably more prominent in the Davies manuscript than in the poem as Shelley published it. *Shadow* is used instead of *Spirit* in line 13, *shade* instead of *light* in line 32 and instead of *power* in line 78.

15. Cronin (129), concludes that, because Julian has not become educated by his confrontation with the Maniac, his earlier faith in humanity has been replaced at the poem's end by a distrust of most people. Scrivener (186), is less absolute but argues that Julian's 'selfish decision' to leave 'illustrates how even an idealist can fail to act in a manner sufficiently utopian'. Hirsch (31–4) sees Julian as a hypocrite because he does not put his theory into practice and Maddalo as a possible redemptive force because he provides for the maniac when others abandon him.

16. Based on this premise, Wilson's argument appears to conclude that *Prometheus Unbound* is nonsense; Wilson asserts that the ideal it portrays 'is attainable only in a realm radically different from the mortal world we inhabit' (88).

17. See Hall (73): '. . . The Imagination is not pure but contingent, not wholly artistic but also moral. To create a world implies the creation of a relationship with another, and to transform a world implies the transformation of one's conduct toward another.'

18. King-Hele (220–7) shows how, through all the permutations of imagery and form in the poem, Shelley maintains a scientifically accurate perspective.

19. Though she neglects or is undecided about thought's pre-eminence in the poem, Chernaik (*Lyrics*, 126) correctly identifies 'the sphere of analogy to human life' as the poem's evolving subject.

20. Bloom (*Visionary Company*, 304) points out that this is a prayer for confrontation of relationship, not for escape.

CHAPTER 3: THE EMPHASIS ON LOVE

1. Shelley, *Complete Poetical Works* (57).

2. Cameron (*Golden Years*, 230) shows how some comments by Peacock about the poem's title have been misleading.
3. Wasserman (*Shelley*, 15–44) deals with the narrator's identifying himself as belonging to the elemental brotherhood. Though aware that the motif of love dominates the invocation and that the narrator is concerned with love, Wasserman (quite arbitrarily, it seems to me) defines the narrator's love as somehow incomplete or limited by his brotherhood with the other components of human existence.
4. Though not developing the concept very far, Steinman declares that the narrator 'seems to embody love properly directed', that he 'appears to be the positive model of love' (256).
5. Hall comments, 'In fact, we could say that the Poet himself now is a kind of image, instead of a maker of images' (27).
6. I like the phrase that Strickland (153) uses to express the cause of the Poet's disorientation: 'an obliteration of nature in vision'.
7. Wasserman (*Shelley*, 36), finding the close of the poem to be phrased as a wish for endless life on earth, suggests that for the narrator, whom he sees as totally world-satisfied, there is no alternative but such a wish. The narrator's cry to share the lot of the Wandering Jew (675–7) is, however, only one of his expressions of frustration because of the Poet's having failed to see life's true potentiality.
8. Cronin (241) notes the achievement of this transition in the poem's fifth stanza.
9. For a discussion of the religious quality in this portion of the ode, see Webb (37–9).
10. Chayes (73) asserts that the speaker finally is more than an instrument, that 'his is the voice that speaks'.
11. As Woodring explains, 'The poet offers to submit his own selfhood to the fierce spirit of renovation' (227).
12. The image in 'Ode to the West Wind' of 'old palaces and towers / Quivering within the wave's intenser day' (33–4) is particularly recalled in the lines,

> And where within the surface of the River
> The shadows of the temples lie
> And never are erased – but tremble ever
> Like things which every cloud can doom to die . . .

> (513–16)

13. I do not mean to disparage analyses such as Cameron's 'Planet-Tempest Passage', which explores the poem's autobiographical images and parallels – aspects that need to be acknowledged. I do, however, object to an insistence that the autobiographical framework constitutes all that is of major importance in the poem.
14. Letters dated 16 April 1821 and 16 July 1821. For a discussion of Shelley's bringing about a change in Byron's evaluation of Keats, see Robinson (163–70).
15. Keats, *Poetical Works* (242) 3.113–18. All line references to the poetry of Keats pertain to this edition.

16. Focusing primarily on the earlier stanzas of *Adonais*, Becht (194–7) uses the terms 'mental events' and 'mental world' to emphasize the reality and primacy of thought in the sphere of the entire poem's concern.

17. The concept, as well as the expression, is in essence that of Keats's relatively neglected poem 'On Death':

> Can Death be sleep, when life is but a dream,
> And scenes of bliss pass as a phantom by?
> The transient pleasures as a vision seem,
> And yet we think the greatest pain's to die.
>
> How strange it is that man on earth should roam,
> And lead a life of woe, but not forsake
> His rugged path; nor dare he view alone
> His future doom which is but to awake.

Since this poem was not published until long after the deaths of Keats and Shelley, the accuracy with which Shelley, in stanza 39 and in subsequent lines, reflects Keats's view of life and death is remarkable.

18. Keach's discussion of the line 'Destroying [*or* Seeking] life alone not peace', from Shelley's late lyric 'Lines Written in the Bay of Lerici', suggests an instance of Shelley's continuing to use disparagingly the term *life* as connoting the 'mad trance' that deprives human beings of peace. As in *Adonais*, the implication of the line seems to be that the *life* that is either destroyed or sought has nothing to do with *peace* – which, after all, is a term readily equated with the true life summed up in the term *love* as it is used in stanza 44 of *Adonais*.

19. Wasserman (*Subtler Language*, 338–9) argues convincingly that the poem does not end with the poet's being attracted to suicide.

20. Cameron (*Golden Years*, 444) interprets the 'abode' of the 'Eternals' as 'the "Senate" of "the Poets," the immortality of intellectual being'. And he explains: 'Like Keats, Shelley will become part of the collective chain of creative intellect that has moved mankind upward through the centuries.'

21. As Scrivener asserts, 'The divinity celebrated in *Adonais*'s third part is alternately human and natural, the product of past and present Poets, but it is not anything even close to the "heaven" of Christian mythology' (280).

CHAPTER 4: THE EMPHASIS ON SOCIAL ENLIGHTENMENT

1. Shaw (248–59) presents an account of old Chartists' testimonies regarding the effect that *Queen Mab* had on their movement.

2. Cameron (*Young Shelley*, 254) provides a valuable comment on the poetic quality and effectiveness of *Queen Mab*: 'If at times the language, in its revolutionary bluntness, short-circuits finer aesthetic transmuta-

tions, its cascading sincerity gives it a rugged intensity of power unique in English poetry. In spite of the higher harmonies and soaring visionariness of *Prometheus Unbound*, *Queen Mab*, dealing with the same theme, cannot simply be regarded as a juvenile precursor. It is a great poem in its own right.'

3. Quoted from Shelley's Notes on *Queen Mab*; see *Poetical Works* (812).
4. Woodring (247–9) suggests that Shelley, in his zealous opposition to orthodox Christianity, overlooks certain factors that, on strictly philosophical grounds, would limit the validity of his argument regarding free will. Nevertheless, in terms of the relationship of thought and art to life, the relevancy of Shelley's point is undiminished.
5. *Poetical Works* (32). All references to *The Revolt of Islam* (page references in regard to the Preface, line references in regard to the poetry) pertain to this edition.
6. Cronin (97, 102–7) suggests that Laon and Cythna are intended as corrections not of Robespierre or Napoleon but of Southey, Landor, Coleridge and Wordsworth, who all experienced an early enthusiasm for the French Revolution but abandoned their revolutionary ideals when the actions of revolutionaries in France became excessive and, in their turn, despotic.
7. See Coleridge, 'Conciones ad Populum, or Address to the People' in *Selected Poetry and Prose* (499).
8. At the request of Ollier, Shelley's publisher, who had received a strong protest from a long-time customer, the poem, originally titled *Laon and Cythna*, was altered so as to remove the originally intended blood relationship between the two lovers. For a concise account of Shelley's discomfort regarding this and other alterations, see Holmes (*Shelley*, 389–91).
9. Later, when Cythna has convinced her audience of the need to end the system of male domination, there are those who sneeringly say that, the rule of men being now over, 'the subject world to woman's will must bow' (3612). Strongly opposed to the whole concept of any group's tyrannizing over another, Cythna terms these people 'obscener slaves' than those who laud the old times of tyranny.
10. See Young (81–4) for a comprehensive discussion of the episode (2443–51) in which Laon and others in a trapped and desperate situation use 'rude pikes' for defence.
11. It is not accurate to say, as does Dawson (75), that 'the conclusions of Shelley's revolutionary epic are, in fact profoundly anti-revolutionary'. Perhaps Dawson means to say that these conclusions are profoundly in opposition to conventional, violent means of revolution and that they support instead a new, revolutionary means of revolution. The new way that Shelley suggests would, in anticipation of Thoreau, Gandhi and King, place the force of human spirit above material force in the campaign for the renovation of society.
12. Woodring shows (266–7) that, although it appears that Hope expects to be trampled by Murder, Fraud and Anarchy, she actually throws herself in their path in 'clear-eyed prescience'. McNiece (*Revolutionary Idea*, 64n) notes a parallel between the maiden Hope and the hope

that Demogorgon extols in the final speech of *Prometheus Unbound*.

13. Woodring (266) identifies the Shape as 'active love' and, further, as 'the solidarity of action through fraternal love'.

14. The view of McNiece (*Revolutionary Idea*, 65) that this repeated stanza 'sounds much more like a call to arms than to wise passiveness' is beside the point and misleading. Certainly, Shelley does not favour passive *non*-resistance; he energetically supports nonviolent *resistance* or what might be called non-violent contention. Lions rising after slumber may be presumed to be enjoying strong control of their turf, not necessarily springing into violent attack.

15. Fischer, relating that followers of Gandhi recalled his reading 'The Mask of Anarchy' at a gathering in India, quotes lines 319–22 and 340–7 of the poem (49).

16. Young deals in some detail with Gandhi's response to Shelley (see especially 19–33, 143–6) and refers also to Thoreau and King.

17. Curran (*Annus Mirabilis*, 174–5) sees the poem's imagery of the sun to be linked with liberty, the storm-cloud imagery linked with tyranny and religion – the latter of these imageries being a man-made parody of the covering shelter provided by the sun's light.

18. Reiman and Powers do not include the Prologue in their edition. Therefore the line references to it pertain to Shelley's *Poetical Works*.

19. Although Scrivener rightly points out Shelley's desire to draw England into alliance with the Greek cause, he tends to overstate the case when, to a degree diminishing his emphasis on Shelley's advocacy of nonviolent struggle, he declares that the poem is 'designed to promote the Greek war for independence by rallying English public opinion . . .'. (287).

20. See Woodring (317–18): 'Freedom belongs to Thought, with its "quick elements" Will, Passion, Reason, and Imagination. Thought cannot die; freedom therefore is immortal. As thought cannot die, eternal Necessity works through it rather than through matter.'

CHAPTER 5: COMPREHENSIVENESS AND SYNTHESIS

1. As Shelley declares in the Preface (133), the work draws its imagery largely 'from the operations of the human mind'.

2. Asia says this in the context of telling Demogorgon that she knows about Saturn's having come to the point of withholding knowledge, power, skill, thought, self-empire and love – thus causing earth's primal spirits to become faint and bringing about the situation in which Prometheus gave power to Jupiter.

3. Baker (95) comments that Jupiter's having kept 'faithless faith' has been a matter of his abandoning love and law, as is typical of the Shelleyan tyrant.

4. Webb (218) deals with influences of Euripides on *Prometheus Unbound* – including mention of Shelley's knowledge of Euripides' *Hercules Furens*, in which Amphitryon speaks of Zeus as 'a rather stupid god or else unjust'.

5. As Woodring makes clear (284), Prometheus has not yet, at this early point, attained the love requisite to renewal.

6. See Baker (113): 'Prometheus' granting Jupiter dominance upon only one condition, namely, that man is to be free, means in effect that the mind of man suffered its fierce wants and mad disquietudes to assume command, while at the same time retaining the power of freedom of choice. Mind may at any time shake off these agonies if the inward conditions of that mind can be made right.'

7. See Byron's 'Prometheus' in his *Poetical Works* (98). Byron ends his poem by drawing a parallel between the human spirit and the spirit of Prometheus:

> Triumphant where it dares defy,
> And making Death a Victory.

8. Bowra (121), in an otherwise enlightening discussion, misinterprets Prometheus' withdrawal of the curse as his forgiveness of Jupiter.

9. See an explanation of the concept in my note in *ELN*, 13 (1975) 25–7.

10. See Wasserman, *Subtler Language* (328–39).

11. Woodman (149, 156–7) finds Shelley accepting a limitation in life on earth that must be endured until the full consummation in the 'intense inane' after death. I, however, read this passage and the concluding speech of Demogorgon as depicting the genuine living encounter that makes of human life in the realm of love something truly vital, rather than a means of biding time until death provides a way of slipping off into the inane.

12. Kurtz (165–6, 189–90) sees the struggle and victory in *Prometheus Unbound* as taking place not in society but entirely within the individual. In Shelley's view, however, such a demarcation in the realm of love is impossible. The conversion of Prometheus does occur within the individual, but its very occurrence makes him one with all that may be called society. Perhaps the best example of this concept in literature other than Shelley's is Oothoon in Blake's *Visions of the Daughters of Albion*. Having plucked the flower and thenceforth living in the life of unity with all, she yet calls to Theotormon and to Albion's daughters who, too, must experience her liberty. So long as they are not transformed, she remains a kind of Prometheus awaiting liberation after his victory over hatred and vengeance.

13. Oras (247–57), while making a good case for Shelley's consciously patterning this passage after portions of *Paradise Lost* and while acknowledging that it was not merely a matter of borrowed imagery but of being spurred on to new invention, does not show *what* Milton stimulated Shelley to invent. To say, as does Oras, that it is an example of 'that concentration to pure form' that Whitehead found to be characteristic of Shelley, is misleading. The *idea* behind the form is here, if anywhere in Shelley, the point of concentration.

14. See Wasserman, *Shelley's Prometheus* (133).

15. Bloom (*Mythmaking*, 275) declares that it is clear that Shelley's myth of relationship is ultimately defeated. In *Visionary Company* (361–2)

Bloom finds in the fragmentary poem's final lines an expression of Shelley's conclusion that life is an ironic cycle, from which follows the poet's going forth 'to seek a sea change'.

16. Rubin (362) suggests that this passage moves us to identify the narrator 'not with the daylight, but with the stars that gem the cone of night'.

17. Abrams (441) defines *life*, as it is used in 'The Triumph of Life', as 'those material and sensual conditions of everyday existence which solicit, depress, and corrupt the aspiring human spirit'.

18. Cronin (218–19) identifies the poem's predominant recurring metaphor as the sun's extinction of a star, but he sees it (222) only as the primary expression of the poem's 'labyrinthine inconclusiveness'.

19. Bloom (*Mythmaking*, 266–72), in a careful reading of the 'shape all light' passage, corrects some misreadings by other critics.

Bibliography

Abrams, M. H., *Natural Supernaturalism: Tradition and Revolution in Romantic Literature* (New York: Norton, 1971).

Baker, Carlos, *Shelley's Major Poetry: the Fabric of a Vision* (1948; New York: Russel & Russell, 1961).

Becht, Ronald E., 'Shelley's *Adonais*: Formal Design and the Lyric Speaker's Crisis of Imagination', *Studies in Philology*, 78 (1981) 194–210.

Blake, William, *Visions of the Daughters of Albion* in *The Poetry and Prose of William Blake*, ed. David V. Erdman (Garden City, NY: Doubleday, 1968).

Bloom, Harold, *Shelley's Mythmaking* (1959; Ithaca: Cornell University Press, 1969).

——, *The Visionary Company: a Reading of English Romantic Poetry* (1961; rev. edn Ithaca: Cornell University Press, 1971).

Bowra, C. M., *The Romantic Imagination* (Cambridge, Mass.: Harvard University Press, 1949).

Brown, Norman O., 'The Prophetic Tradition', *Studies in Romanticism*, 21 (1982) 367–86.

Byron, George Gordon, Lord, *Poetical Works* (London: Oxford University Press, 1967).

Cameron, Kenneth Neill, 'Shelley as Philosophical and Social Thinker: Some Modern Evaluations', *Studies in Romanticism*, 21 (1982) 357–66.

——, *Shelley: the Golden Years* (Cambridge, Mass.: Harvard University Press, 1974).

——, 'The Planet–Tempest Passage in *Epipsychidion*', *PMLA*, 63 (1948) 950–72.

——, *The Young Shelley: Genesis of a Radical* (New York: Macmillan, 1950).

Chayes, Irene H., 'Rhetoric as Drama: An Approach to the Romantic Ode', *PMLA*, 79 (1964) 67–79.

Chernaik, Judith, *The Lyrics of Shelley* (Cleveland, Ohio: Press of Case Western Reserve University, 1972).

——, 'Textual Emandations for Three Poems by Shelley', *Keats–Shelley Journal*, 19 (1970) 41–8.

——, and Timothy Burnett, 'The Byron and Shelley Notebooks in the Scrope Davies Find', *Review of English Studies*, 29 (1978) 36–49.

Coleridge, Samuel Taylor, *Selected Poetry and Prose*, ed. Elizabeth Schneider (2nd edn San Francisco: Rinehart, 1971).

Cronin, Richard, *Shelley's Poetic Thoughts* (New York: St. Martin's, 1981).

Curran, Stuart, *Shelley's Cenci: Scorpions Ringed with Fire* (Princeton University Press, 1970).

——, *Shelley's Annus Mirabilis: the Maturing of an Epic Vision* (San Marino, Calif.: Huntington Library, 1975).

——, 'Shelley's Emandations to the *Hymn to Intellectual Beauty*', *English Language Notes*, 7 (1970) 41–8.

Dawson, P. M. S., *The Unacknowledged Legislator: Shelley and Politics* (New York and London: Oxford University Press, 1980).

Duerksen, Roland A., 'Shelley's "Deep Truth" Reconsidered', *English Language Notes*, 13 (1975) 25–7.

Fischer, Louis, *Gandhi: His Life and Message for the World* (New York: Mentor–NAL, 1954).

Grabo, Carl, *The Magic Plant: the Growth of Shelley's Thought* (Chapel Hill: University of North Carolina Press, 1936).

Hall, Jean, *The Transforming Image: a Study of Shelley's Major Poetry* (Urbana: University of Illinois Press, 1980).

Hirsch, Bernard A., '"A Want of That True Theory": *Julian and Maddalo* as Dramatic Monologue', *Studies in Romanticism*, 17 (1978) 13–34.

Hoagwood, Terrence Allan, *Prophecy and the Philosophy of Mind: Traditions of Blake and Shelley* (University of Alabama Press, 1985).

Holmes, Richard, 'Scrope's Last Throw', *Harper's* (Apr. 1977) 77–85.

——, *Shelley: the Pursuit* (New York: Dutton, 1975).

Hymes, Barbaranell, 'Shelley, Byron Papers – Literary Gold They Aren't', *Christian Science Monitor* (16 Mar. 1977) 27.

Keach, William, *Shelley's Style* (New York and London: Methuen, 1984).

Keats, John, *Poetical Works*, ed. H. W. Garrod (London: Oxford University Press, 1966).

King-Hele, Desmond, *Shelley: the Man and the Poet* (New York: Thomas Yoseloff, 1960).

Knerr, Anthony D., *Shelley's Adonais: a Critical Edition* (New York: Columbia University Press, 1984).

Kurtz, Benjamin P., *The Pursuit of Death* (New York: Oxford University Press, 1933).

McGann, Jerome J., *The Romantic Ideology: a Critical Investigation* (University of Chicago Press, 1983).

McNiece, Gerald, 'The Poet as Ironist in "Mont Blanc" and "Hymn to Intellectual Beauty"', *Studies in Romanticism*, 14 (1975) 311–36.

——, *Shelley and the Revolutionary Idea* (Cambridge, Mass: Harvard University Press, 1969).

Oras, Ants, 'The Multitudinous Orb: Some Miltonic Elements in Shelley', *Modern Language Quarterly*, 16 (1955) 247–57.

Perkins, David, *The Quest for Permanence: the Symbolism of Wordsworth, Shelley, and Keats* (Cambridge, Mass.: Harvard University Press, 1959).

Pulos, C. E., *The Deep Truth: a Study of Shelley's Scepticism* (Lincoln: University of Nebraska Press, 1954).

Reiman, Donald H., *Percy Bysshe Shelley* (New York: Twayne, 1969).

——, *Shelley's 'The Triumph of Life': a Critical Study* (Urbana: University of Illinois Press, 1965).

Rieder, John, 'Shelley's Mont Blanc: Landscape and the Ideology of the Sacred Text', *ELH*, 48 (1981) 778–98.

Robinson, Charles E., *Shelley and Byron: the Snake and the Eagle Wreathed in Fight* (Baltimore: Johns Hopkins University Press, 1976).

Rogers, Neville, 'The Scrope Davies "Shelley Find"', *Keats–Shelley Memorial Bulletin*, 28 (1977) 1–9.

Rubin, Merle R., 'Shelley's Skepticism: A Detachment Beyond Despair', *Philological Quarterly*, 59 (1980) 353–73.

Scrivener, Michael Henry, *Radical Shelley: The Philosophical Anarchism and Utopian Thought of Percy Bysshe Shelley* (Princeton University Press, 1982).

Shaw, George Bernard, *Pen Portraits and Reviews* in *Collected Works*, ed. Eyot St. Lawrence (New York: William H. Wise, 1932).

Shelley, Percy Bysshe, *The Complete Poetical Works*, ed. Thomas Hutchinson (London: Oxford University Press, 1943).

——, *The Letters of Percy Bysshe Shelley*, vol. 2, ed. Frederick L. Jones (Oxford University Press, 1964) 2 vols.

——, *Shelley's Poetry and Prose*, eds Donald H. Reiman and Sharon B. Powers (New York: Norton, 1977).

——, *Shelley's Prose: or The Trumpet of a Prophecy*, ed. David Lee Clark (Albuquerque: University of New Mexico Press, 1954).

Sperry, Stuart M., 'Necessity and the Role of the Hero in Shelley's *Prometheus Unbound*', *PMLA*, 96 (1981) 242–54.

Steinman, Lisa M., 'Shelley's Skepticism: Allegory in *Alastor*', *ELH*, 45 (1978) 255–69.

Strickland, Edward, 'Transfigured Night: the Visionary Inversions of *Alastor*', *Keats–Shelley Journal*, 33 (1984) 148–60.

Wasserman, Earl R., *Shelley: a Critical Reading* (Baltimore: Johns Hopkins University Press, 1971).

——, *Shelley's Prometheus Unbound: a Critical Reading* (Baltimore: Johns Hopkins University Press, 1965).

——, *The Subtler Language: Critical Readings of Neoclassic and Romantic Poems* (Baltimore: Johns Hopkins University Press, 1959).

Webb, Timothy, *Shelley: a Voice Not Understood* (Manchester University Press, 1977).

White, Harry, 'Relative Means and Ends in Shelley's Social–Political Thought', *Studies in English Literature*, 22 (1982) 613–31.

Wilson, James D., 'Beatrice Cenci and Shelley's Vision of Moral Responsibility', *Ariel*, 9 (1978) 75–89.

Woodman, Ross Greig, *The Apocalyptic Vision in the Poetry of Shelley* (University of Toronto Press, 1964).

Woodring, Carl, *Politics in English Romantic Poetry* (Cambridge, Mass.: Harvard University Press, 1970).

Wordsworth, William, *Selected Poems and Prefaces*, ed. Jack Stillinger (Boston: Houghton Mifflin, 1965).

Wright, John W., *Shelley's Myth of Metaphor* (Athens: University of Georgia Press, 1970).

Young, Art, *Shelley and Nonviolence* (The Hague: Mouton, 1975).

Index